ARRIVING IN THE WORLD!

Being born is a very peculiar experience. I was just having this lovely dream about the wonderful dark cave that I'd got really rather attached to when I felt an urge to see if there was anywhere else in the world. After a lot of shouting of 'Push, push, you're doing great!' accompanied by strange breathing noises – pop there I was! Out in this other place that was definitely not a dark cave but a huge space with bright lights and lots of people wearing strange clothes talking loudly and waving things, saying something about Apgar tests and numbers, and poking me with certain things and prodding me with others. What it was all about I hadn't the foggiest, but they seemed very determined to pick me up and weigh me and then shout excitedly about the numbers.

Finally, the vast swathes of medical people seemed satisfied with the various numerals and suddenly there he was. Staring right at me. A big head with lots of black hair, dark eyebrows, unnaturally white teeth, an utterly soppy expression on his face and tears in his eyes. Who was this?

He started to talk to me about how he never knew how much love and pride he would feel blah blah… and told me how he liked me even better than Squiddly and Diddly, whoever they are (dogs, I discovered later). And then I clicked. This was the voice I'd been hearing all that time in the cave, going on about Sinitta – who? – pop charts – what? – having the X factor – why? Yes, this was Dad!

He looked alright, and as long as I'm top dog when compared with his actual dogs, that's OK.

I started looking around hopefully for that lovely lady whose voice I'd heard even more often than Dad's, and angling for a morsel of food, but had no luck – it was photo time instead. On Dad's chest no less, once someone had restrained my undercarriage, that is, with a bit of white paper stuck together with some Velcro. It's called a nappy apparently, and is very undignified IMHO.

So while a bunch of people gathered round with bits and pieces of machinery with lenses on the ends of them, Dad grabbed me and snuggled me into his chest hair. This wasn't quite the chest I had in mind, but I waited patiently while the cameras clicked around me, capturing snaps of my nappy-enclosed bottom and the drippy expression on Dad's face. Then Dad reached for another machine, his 'phone', and pressed lots of buttons and it made lots of beeps. I found out later that he was putting the nicest photo of him and me on something called Twitter for his followers, or 'twits' as I call them.

It seemed to me at this point that proceedings had been dragging on for long enough, and it was pretty much now that I began to beg, most pitifully, for a spot of dinner. OK, I screamed blue murder.

It worked! I was handed over to the lovely lady I'd been waiting to meet – Mum! She looked a tad on the tired side. I don't know why she should be tired when clearly Dad had been the one on his feet for hours, saying encouraging things to her on top of dashing on and off various planes to get here on time, which must have been even more tiring. But she was defo totes amazeballs, and more importantly, she had food and plenty of it! I tucked straight in – good stuff this breast milk, I can tell you – and then I settled down to a nice postprandial nap.

I woke up to find that everyone was all of a twitter. By which I mean that Dad's twits and almost the whole world was going crazy with the news that I had been born. Quite right! I'm sure that when everyone is born they think they are the centre of the universe, and with me it turned out to be true. I guessed that at some point I'd find out why.

I got some clues when eventually we left this place called the hospital to go to somewhere called 'home'. I was hoping it would be small and cosy, just like my lovely cave. Cave, ah well…

So, I got manhandled by Dad into what he called the car seat while he said things like 'OK, my wuvvely, buvvely little man, it's off home now for us, you bootiful, bootiful little baba', and utter equivalent unconscionable rubbish. Gosh, grown-ups don't half talk rot. And then we left the hospital to go to something else called the car. I say then we left. What I actually mean is that Mum and Dad and several other people then spent about three hours picking up bags and saying things like 'Do you have the muslins?' 'No, I thought you had them' and 'No, I've just got the bibs and the dummies.' 'OK, well, look in the Prada yummy-mummy changing bag they might be in there', 'I did but they're not...' etc., etc., until I screamed blue murder again and that concentrated minds wonderfully. Finally we made it out to the car.

Well, we made it outside to where there were about sixteen rows of people pointing more cameras at us. Mum and Dad were very concerned I shouldn't be screaming uncontrollably at this point, so Mum had given me a big yummy load of milk before we left, which put me in a rather woozy state, you know how it is, and the whole thing of the cameras and the flashes and the shouting of the names 'Simon!' 'Lauren!' – why I don't know – passed in a rather pleasing blur. Off home to the lovely cave. Daddy says it's really nice.

This isn't a cave! It's huge! And it's full of swimming pools, and bright lights, and no carpets, and nothing dark and homey, and if I were to sum it up in one word, that word would be 'bling'. Bear in mind, I've no idea what bling means but if it means anything, it means this.

Daddy says it has the X factor.

AT HOME

And if I thought I'd already met quite a lot of people and maybe life could get a bit quieter now, I thought wrong. Nestling in among the big enormous plasma screens, the telephones everywhere and the white sofas were hordes more people. So there were not one, not two, but three lovely ladies who picked me up whenever Daddy let go of me, which wasn't often, and squeezed me into uncomfortable things they called 'super-cute clothes', and dangled me around the place, saying such rubbish as, 'dere, dere, lubbly little fing, oo don't need to cwy so much, s'awlright, little darling, everyfing's awlright.' When plainly it wasn't, otherwise I wouldn't be crying, would I? Stands to reason, dunnit!

And then I met Jeeves. Well, Daddy called him Piers, but I call him Jeeves. And he always wears smart black clothes and has a different way of talking to everybody else. He is a real cut above. He didn't talk baby rubbish like everyone else; instead he said things like, 'And how would Sir like his nappy done up today? Traditional classic fit or a little more snug around the middle for Sir, perhaps?' It was very refreshing. I resolved to ask him for a Scotch on the rocks, just as soon as I could work up the vocabulary.

I was just having a bit of quiet time with Mum when a strange electronic noise cut through the air with the terrifying words: 'So macho! He's gotta be so macho!' sung over and over again. What in the world was that?! Well, guess what, it's the ring-tone of Daddy's phone (of course, what did you expect?) and during the afternoon he was very busy answering the phone to people and inviting them to come and see me. And then Jeeves was very busy opening the door to one after another of Daddy's friends, and I can tell you, there were a lot of them! They all arrived with a variety of stuffed animals in various shades of blue, grey and white – what's wrong with a bit of red or pink, I want to know? Lots of them brought flowers too and big bottles of stuff that I'm not allowed to drink, it seems. They all sounded very excited and they all wanted to see – me!

My favourite was the little man with the funny voice (Jeeves told me in confidence that he was Irish) who said to me, 'You're the one to beat in this competition and that's a fact', which I thought was rather strange as I wasn't aware that my life was a competition. I also liked Harry Bighair who said, 'Yeah!' a lot as well as 'Wow!' and 'Cool!'

It appears that I was born on something called Valentine's Day. So Harry Bighair asked Daddy if he was going to call me Valentino. Daddy answered, 'I'm not going to dignify that with a reply.' But he did anyway, saying, 'Not in a billion years. There's only so many words I can drag out of my vocabulary to say how awful that idea is.' Sometimes I wish Daddy would speak his mind more often and not just sit on the fence all the time.

Meanwhile, I've found out what Daddy's name is – Simon is what everyone says to him, so I think that's his name. And Mummy is Lauren. So they have names, but what about me? Daddy said he was going to call me Simon too, but I think that would have been a very bad idea as everyone would have got confused, especially me. So instead he tells everybody that I am Eric, which was Daddy's daddy's name, although that must be very confusing for Daddy's mummy.

When some of Daddy's friends had gone and there were only about twenty people in my home rather than fifty as there had been up till then, Daddy sat down and put me on his chest again and told me about the name Eric. He said Eric is a great name because it means 'eternal ruler' and 'ever powerful' and 'ruler of the people'. Coooool! Does that mean I can demand whatever I want whenever I want it? Yes, I think it does! Bearing this in mind I concluded it was, as ever, time for a mid-afternoon snack. I called politely to Mum to suggest a spot of liquid refreshment. Yup, I was screaming myself silly again. And it worked! Just about thirty seconds of violent yelling and Mum took me off to an enormous room with a huge bed in it covered in cushions, and gave me a drop of the good stuff. Truly, I am the ruler of the people! And, more importantly – milk!

Well, my first day out of hospital was nearly over when Daddy said there were two more 'members of the family' he needed to introduce to me. These turned out to be rather like so many of the stuffed creatures everyone had been bringing us all day long, with one very remarkable exception. They moved! And I don't just mean moved a little bit like 'Lily Ladybird' or the equally facile 'Freddy Frog', I mean they basically never stopped moving. And they were seriously furry. And the noises they made! Blimey, they were almost louder than me, or Daddy, and that's saying something.

I found out they are dogs – Yorkshire Terriers, to be precise. One is called Squiddly and one is called Diddly, but don't ask me which is which. Mum says it's even harder than working out which one is Ant and which one is Dec, whatever that means. Squiddly is meant to always be on the left side so everyone will know it's him, but of course he always moves, so that doesn't work. I wonder if Ant and Dec have the same problem. Also one of them, I think it's Squiddly, seems to have a serious bladder problem – he needs to wee more often even than I do. I don't know if Ant or Dec has that issue, too.

Anyway, they're alright, I suppose. Nice and furry, but I told Jeeves in no uncertain terms that I intend to be number-one priority in this house and there's to be no putting those dogs before me. No siree! Jeeves muttered something darkly about Daddy having said before I was born that he was worried he would love the dogs more than me, but now that I was out and about he didn't feel that way any more and I was definitely top of the pile. I tried to thank Jeeves for providing me with this remarkably excellent potential emotional blackmail material on Dad, but I'm not sure he grasped the subtlety of my speech, as his response, 'Shhh, there, don't cry' was not wholly commensurate with what I'd been trying to convey.

Then just to round off a perfect day, Dad got more people with more cameras to take photos of me with my new 'friends' Ridiculous Knitted Elephant and Overly Cutie Dog, as I call them, stuffed up next to me. As if this photo existing wasn't bad enough, he then posted the picture on Twitter for all of his twits to see, and anyone else in the world who fancied looking. I mean how embarrassing is that going to be when I am grown up and applying for a job as an accountant? Honestly, parents these days just don't think things through. I tried pointing this out to Jeeves, but unfortunately, although I am sure we are on the same wavelength really, he didn't seem to get my drift and instead merely replied, 'Yes, Eric, I couldn't agree more. Let me see if I can find someone to sort out that wind for you', which really wasn't what I'd been driving at.

I decided to make the best of a bad job and turn in for a night of sleeping like a baby, i.e. I wake up every two hours, screaming for milk.

LIFE'S A BEACH

So, today I went to the beach for the first time with Mummy, Daddy, Squiddly and Diddly, Jeeves and about sixteen other people. I only had eyes for Mummy and Daddy, but Squiddly or Diddly – or rather, Ant and Dec, as I have decided to call them – only had eyes for me. There I was, happily lounging away in a specially built beach tent designed to keep the sun off me, having a nice little doze, when Ant, or Dec, came up and gave me a great big lick on the face. The liberty of it! And everyone was too busy chatting to notice for ages. Finally Jeeves spotted what was happening and ran over to assist me and shoo Ant firmly away. Or possibly Dec. Quite right too.

'What's wrong, Piers?' said Daddy. Jeeves told him all about the dreaded Yorkshire Terrier face-lick incident and Daddy replied, 'Oh, that's fine. Edward said that's how Squids and Dids would bond with Eric, it's all about smells and licks to them, you see.' Edward is the dog expert Daddy hired to make sure me and Ant and Dec would all get along nicely, like one big happy family and so they wouldn't be jealous of me. Them jealous of me? – what about my feelings in all of this? I am the centre of the universe, I would have them know. I'll give them some smells to contend with if they get in my way, I can tell you.

Next thing I knew, Daddy had Ant and Dec all over his chest – outrageous! That's my spot I think you'll find! I admit I have been rather rude about the virtues of the area, but now some canines are trying to grab it, I have become rather possessive, thank you very much!

I was frankly quite relieved when Daddy went off to walk in the sea and be photographed next to a bunch of barely-clad women – 'beach lovelies', he called them. I snuggled up with Mummy. I don't know what has happened to her lovely food-dispensing system but it's suddenly got an awful plastic taste to it. I didn't kick up too much of a fuss because I didn't want to hurt Mummy's feelings, but, seriously, I think she needs to see a dermatologist if her skin shifts from feeling lovely and soft when we're at home to hard plastic when we're out and about. I must make a mental note to ask Jeeves what it's all about next time we get some quality 'Jeeves and Sir' time.

I thought the beach was pretty great – the best thing about it was that with all the lovely fresh air, and drink from Mum, I spent pretty much the whole day sleeping. Lovely. That was bad news for Mum though, as it meant I would spend the whole night awake… Or it would have done had I not managed to get in a good spot of screaming way before bedtime because of how we got home. Some people drive to the beach, some people walk to the beach, but not us, oh no! We Cowells, we fly to the beach, and home again. A luxury private jet, of course. Or, as Jeeves has renamed it – a jet-powered mobile baby screaming machine.

Ugh – flying is so horrible! First you get strapped into a car seat, with only Ridiculous Knitted Elephant for company, and driven in a car to something called an airport, where there are loads of big machines sat on the ground and lots of people saying, 'This way please, Sir, not that way' and 'Mind the propellors' and such like. Then I get held precariously in Mum's arms as she climbs up some steps with an awful wind whipping past us and noise everywhere. Finally you're inside and get to lie down on a nice sofa and have a look out of a tiny window – and just when you're thinking maybe this isn't so bad after all, your ears are assailed by the most tremendous noise which sounds like the entire world is exploding, and that just gets louder and louder until Jeeves says, 'Sir can relax now, we are airborne, so Sir's screaming could perhaps abate a little.'

Oh could it, indeed, Jeeves? I think not.

Finally the noise stops and then you have to go through the whole palaver again but in reverse – down the steps with the wind and the noise, back into the car seat, with Overly Cutie Dog stuffed next to my face this time, listen while Mummy and Daddy bicker about how much fun it is, or isn't, flying in a private jet with a tiny baby, and at last home.

And Mummy tasted all nice and normal again, not plasticky. Honestly, what's with that?

Before bed, Daddy grabbed me back onto his chest and told me about my other name, my middle name, Phillip. So that name is also named after Daddy's daddy, who I am never going to meet, apparently. Mummy didn't get much of a look into of all of this, it seemed to me. The other reason my middle name is Phillip is because it's the name of one of Daddy's really good friends, Philip Green, who makes clothes Mummy says she wouldn't be seen dead in. So that all makes sense.

Well, another successful day over. Time to retire to my darkened room, comforted only by a whirly thing that whizzes around above my head, making a noise and flashing out lights – why this is meant to be relaxing, I don't know – and occasional visits from Mummy, Daddy, Jeeves and about twenty-seven other people. Actually not Jeeves – he is sensible enough to know that Sir doesn't like to be disturbed when it's bedtime except to be offered a good stiff drink.

Daddy tucked me into bed. 'Nighty, nighty, darling Eric. You know what? You are really, really good, but now it's snoozy-woozy time for all good little babas,' says Daddy. Oh, please.

HOME ALONE

When Daddy and Mummy go out to a restaurant and poor little Eric is left all alone. Well, not exactly alone…

So finally it came to it – I was only a week old and there were my parents gadding off, living the high life, and leaving me all alone with only Jeeves, Ant and Dec, about seventeen members of Mummy's close family and an assortment of stuffed animals to take care of me. Does it really take that many people to look after one baby? I must be one heck of a handful. And if I'm not yet, I should start planning to be, that's for sure.

So Daddy and Mummy went out to a high-class

restaurant. It all happened like this. Mummy said, 'Hey, Sugarpie (Sugarpie?), let's go out to celebrate Eric and you and me with a slap-up feed.' Daddy said, 'Great idea, darling! Come on, let's show everyone how beautiful you still are and how great I look with you, and go out on the town.' And Mummy said, 'What do you mean, how beautiful I "still" am?' And Daddy said, 'Hey, don't go taking things the wrong way now. I just mean even though Eric's been born you're still lovely, and one day you'll have your figure back, I'm sure.' And Mummy said, 'He's only one week old, what do you expect, for Chrissake?' and then crossed herself for blaspheming. And Daddy said, 'Pas devant les domestiques', because he went to a posh boarding school, and even though he hated it some of the French got through by osmosis. And Mummy said, 'What the hell does that mean?!' because she had never managed to get much of a grip on European languages, including English. And Daddy said, 'Now calm down, darling, I just mean…'

At that point Jeeves intervened and whisked me off to a different room, which was a real bother as I was rather enjoying their conversation. But luckily they were talking nice and loudly so I could still hear some of it coming through the walls. Bits like 'You're damn right, you better take me out to dinner and spoil me after that!' from Mummy, and 'At least you're not giving me the silent treatment,' from Daddy. 'Oh no, you can wait for that until we get home', from Mummy, and 'Oh Christ, so is that what I've got to look forward to later?' from Daddy, and then 'Don't you dare swear against God in my presence,' from Mummy, and 'But you did!' from Daddy, and so on.

Jeeves could see from the look in my eyes that I was taking in every word. They say that babies can't understand what's going on. Huh! Various maternity nurses had been busying around grabbing me off Jeeves and singing tunelessly in my ears to distract me, but Jeeves and I caught each other's eye – he could tell I was picking up everything – and shared a good little chuckle between us.

He's a man in a million that Jeeves, I tell you.

Finally Mummy and Daddy got back on speaking terms, gave each other lots of smoochy hugs, decided on their various semi-matching clothes and left. But not before giving me lots of sloppy kisses that I could definitely have done without, and receiving manifold reassurances from Jeeves, and other assorted hangers-on, that I would be fine and that they would call Mummy or Daddy on their phones if I did anything untoward – like cry most piteously, presumably. Or suddenly produce the complete works of William Shakespeare on the iPad.

Well I didn't quite bang out the Shakespeare as I'd hoped, but I did cry most piteously. Did Mummy and Daddy come back? Did they heck! Instead I discovered that other people can give me food, too, but the milk they give me has the same terrible plastic taste that Mummy's milk has when she feeds me when we're not at home. What is going on with this? Perhaps at some time I shall find out what the things at the end of my arms are for, and then I will be able to hold things, and perhaps that will help me find out why things are different. So much to do, so much to find out!

But for now, time for a lot of pointless lying about,

crying and then going to sleep, followed shortly by wetting my pants. Oh yep, my agenda is pretty much full up with that for now.

THE COWELL LOOK

Dawn arrived bright and clear and I celebrated with a good deal of loud waaahing that brought everybody running. Actually I had had a good old waah a bunch of times before dawn too, mainly to check that Mummy and Daddy had actually come back. Well, Mummy was around, but I didn't see Daddy until several hours later. I don't know why that was, but Mummy gave me a clue when she said, 'You've not gone back to work yet, you know. You can just about get up to look after Eric in the night as often as me.' Daddy replied to this with a snore. But a little later he was up and about, talking on the telephone, typing on the telephone, shouting on the telephone and texting on the telephone. I think he was trying to show he was busy 'working'.

Then, in a sudden dramatic twist of events, he volunteered to change my undercarriage garments for the first time. I had just had a nice wee, which was very comforting and relieving, when I found Dad's arms around me, saying, 'Come on, little man, I'm going to sort you out with a brand new nappy, oh yes I am.' Okaaay, let's see how this works out. Daddy has much bigger hands than Mummy. And seriously hairy arms. Mummy stood next to Daddy, while Jeeves watched subtly from one corner of the room, and I spotted one of the maternity nurses sneakily catching a reflection of the events from a mirror while standing in the hallway, a small smirk on her face. I'm not sure why.

First step: nappy off. Yep, he managed that. Then the clean up – pretty unnecessary, as it was only a wee, but there's no point trying to explain that to new parents. Then a new nappy on. 'Nice and tight,' said Daddy. 'And nice and high,' he added. 'Yes, almost up to my shoulder blades!' I thought. 'Hey, steady on there! How high do you think my waist actually is!'

'Like father, like son,' murmured Mummy, suppressing a giggle. 'I don't know what you mean!'

said Daddy, going a peculiar shade of red. But evidently the maternity nurses knew what she meant as their muffled laughter delighted the air. Luckily Jeeves breezed over to diffuse proceedings: 'It's almost time for your television interview,' he said to Daddy, and expertly picking me up, discreetly managed to lower the nappy to an almost sensible height. Daddy quickly planted a great sloppy kiss on my head and disappeared from view, calling out, 'Duty calls! Gotta run!'

He came back later, just in time to wake me up from a lovely sleep by taking a shower and making some extraordinary noises – I think he believed it to be a form of 'singing'. Dear God, I can't imagine anyone else would have called it that. Daddy has said that somebody else's singing sounded like Mickey Mouse on helium. Well, this was more like Minnie Mouse on valium. Truly frightful. Well, never mind, the show I put on as a consequence got me some illicit midnight milk, so I don't care.

THE BABY WEARS PRADA

Daddy took me out in the buggy today for the first time. It was really fun! The whole process of leaving our home took about six hours while Mummy packed and re-packed the Prada changing bag several times, saying things like, 'Are you sure you know what you're doing?' and 'You will make sure the eye shade is covering his eyes, won't you? He mustn't have any direct sunlight on him, you know.' And 'Don't push the buggy too fast, will you, it could give him a tummy ache.' There was a great kerfuffle as some white stuff was got out of the fridge and poured into plastic things and Mummy was very particular about it, saying things like 'It nearly killed me to make those eight ounces of that, so don't you dare spill it' and 'Are you really sure you will be OK on your own with little darling Eric Werick?' Eric Werick? – honestly!

Well, Daddy answered, 'Hey, how hard can it be? I've managed the biggest pop band in the world, so I think I can manage one baby.' That sounds like an invitation to cause trouble. I'll have to see what I can do.

Jeeves raised an eyebrow, just one infinitesimal degree, and I could tell he could see what I was thinking, but of course he is the soul of discretion. He merely said to Daddy, 'Would Sir's Sir (that is what he calls Daddy. I know – LOL!) like me to cover Eric in his Special Blanket?' 'Yes, Piers, thank you.' Jeeves put said Special Blanket over me – 'Pecial Blankie nice and high for Eric,' said Daddy – what is this obsession with him that things should be pulled up nice and high? But at least he didn't say Eric Werick. Then Daddy went a bit pink in the face.

I think there is something funny about this Special Blanket and I'm going to get to the bottom of it soon.

But meanwhile, there was a park trip to be had, and some good old-fashioned mischief. It's OK, I'm just taking after Daddy. Everyone says that he was an absolute tearaway when he was a little boy. Mummy says he still is.

So eventually out we went, just Daddy and me, and the Fendi buggy. Oh, and RKE (Ridiculous Knitted Elephant), Overly Cutie Dog, Pecial Blankie, not forgetting the Prada changing bag stuffed with a multitude of plastic items to make sure my every whim is catered for. Quite right, too.

At first it was very noisy. There were lots of cars and people everywhere. I couldn't see them because all I get to do is lie down and look sideways at RKE or upwards at the sky – and mighty entertaining that is, I can tell you. Blue and everything. But then we arrived somewhere much quieter and I could hear music that was much nicer than the stuff Daddy puts on in the house whenever people are visiting, and much much nicer than those dreadful sounds I heard coming out of Daddy's mouth when he was in the shower. These sounds were soft and ever changing, yet ever constant, too. I saw little creatures hopping

30

about around lovely floaty green things, which I think are leaves on trees. Those must be the birds that Jeeves said I would see in the park, and these sounds must be music. Real music. How lovely! I wonder why Daddy doesn't play these sounds when people visit our house?

Then there were sounds of people coming near to us, talking excitedly and saying things like, 'Hey, is that really Simon Cowell with his new baby? Wow, what a cool guy he is! Out on his own with his new baby! Let's go and say hi.' And so they came over and said hello to Daddy and pointed at me. Daddy had his soppy face on again and smiled big smiles, showing his unnaturally white teeth, and then they all poked their telephones into my buggy and took more photos of me, and photos of Daddy, and asked Daddy to pick me up. So he grabbed me without so much as a by your leave, and they took photos of Daddy holding me. This was all getting rather tiresome and Daddy and I both thought it was time for a change – I was keen on getting some milk, while Daddy wanted to take his top off. Which he did. Then he put me back in the buggy and paraded me around a bit more while other people took photos of Daddy without his top on, pushing me in a buggy. Is that all life is, just a series of photos? It would seem so.

Well, I had had quite enough of this food-free route march and I decided to inform Daddy in no uncertain terms of my overwhelming desire for milk. I began with just a small waah, which he smiled his white teeth at and ignored, then I built up to a more effective volume of waaah, which he ignored with a quick tug at the top of his jeans to hoist them up higher. Why? And finally I reached a crescendo of screaming that couldn't be ignored. It wasn't! Hooray! Daddy's big hands reached into the buggy and prised me away from Overly Cutie, from which I was attempting to derive milk, and sat down on a park bench and began to feed me some of the good stuff.

So Daddy can feed me too! This is good to know! But it does have that awful plasticky taste again. I wonder why. Well, I quickly zipped through the eight ounces and looked around for more. Daddy looked as well, although he looked in the Prada bag, which was probably a more realistic option, whereas I was looking at Daddy's hands, the bench, the trees, anywhere my eyes happened upon really. But neither of us had any luck. Hmm, well, I wasn't going to put up with this. Time for a demonstration. Does Daddy really think I'm going to be as easy to manage as One Direction? I think not.

Suffice it to say, I had Daddy out of that park and back home to Mummy PDQ. And no one saw much of his white teeth on the way back, I can tell you. Fastest way of making him put his top back on I ever saw. I must remember that.

Ah! Back home to Mummy and time for a lovely snuggle. 'Did I want more milky wilky?' she asked, rather incoherently. 'Of course, little Eric Werick (not that again). Little babas need their mamas, don't they?' So she offered me more milk but I decided I didn't really want milk after all. Time for a snooze instead. Mmm... Just before I drifted into a peaceful sleep with milky dreams I saw Daddy grit his bright white teeth and mutter, 'Oh, you're all peaceful and happy now, aren't you, now that no one's watching.' Of course Jeeves was watching, but Daddy says Piers doesn't count.

DADDY ON THE TELLY

I woke up to find that everyone, including Daddy, was watching Daddy on one of the massive TVs. He was talking to a lady called Terri Seymour, who had fallen over and broken her arm in an attempt to have something as interesting happen to her, as had happened to Daddy – i.e. becoming a father to me. Terri asked Daddy what it was like to have me around and Daddy replied that he was born to be a dad. I wondered why it had taken him so long to be one in that case. Mummy didn't look at the screen when Terri was on, I didn't know why. Luckily Jeeves could see my confusion and muttered to me confidentially that Terri and Daddy used to go out together and so that made Mummy a bit cross. I thought he meant they used to go out to the park to hear the lovely bird music, but it seems he didn't mean that either. Daddy clicked the pause button and said it didn't mean a thing any more because he hadn't met the right woman then, but now that he'd met Mummy she was the right woman. And then they got all lovey-dovey and kissy and smoochy and yucky and disgustingy. Hey, what about me?!

A short waah later and I was back where I should be, at the centre of all the attention. Daddy unpaused the television so we could all carry on watching him and Terri asked him if he wanted to have any more babies, and he said yes, another one, or two! Mummy said, 'Easy for you to say, all you had to do was dash from London to New York, and arrive in time to get the glory. Some of us actually had to give birth to him, you know!' 'It's OK, darling, there's no rush,' said Daddy. 'You bet your life there's no rush,' said Mummy. 'And anyway, Eric does already have a brother.' Do I? First I'd heard of it!

And so while Mummy and Daddy started talking louder and louder, and Mummy began picking up plates and spoons and throwing them at Daddy in some kind of funny game in which Daddy was seemingly not supposed to catch them, Jeeves calmly breezed in and escorted me to another sitting room to Explain Things.

So here's the thing. Apparently I have an older brother from when Mummy used to be married to somebody else. So Mummy has had a baby before, but Daddy never has. Goddit! But now Mummy is not married to him any more, because she is married to Daddy, right? Wrong. Mummy and Daddy are not married but it's just like they are married because they love each other very much and they are always going to be together and I mustn't worry. What does that mean – they are always going to be together? They're not always together now. Mummy goes out on her own to buy more clothes and shoes, and more houses to fit the new clothes and shoes into. And Daddy goes into his smoking room and talks on the telephone loudly. And why shouldn't I worry? I had no intention to worry, but now I think maybe I should. I'm not sure about what, but something presumably is worthy of worrying about, no?

But that's not all of it. So the man who Mummy used to be married to says that my Daddy can't see the baby who Mummy had with the man she used to be married to, but who isn't a baby any more. Right, that all makes sense. Er… So, when does Mummy see the baby who isn't a baby any more, and what happens if Daddy walks into the room at the same time? This sounds like a recipe for disaster, or as I call it, an opportunity for a whole bundle of mischief and fun.

Jeeves brought me back in to see Mummy and Daddy, who were at the kissing business once more, while Mummy attached a few plasters to some red bits on Daddy's arms, where he had failed to catch some of the plates and spoons, and then they both dangled me and blew raspberries on my tummy – why? – and Mummy called me her little Eric Werick. And Daddy started singing to me again (no, *please*, God, make it stop!). Then they talked about finding just the right person to look after me when they wanted to go off and do different things, like how Daddy likes to have lots of time so he can talk loudly on the telephone, and time to paint his teeth, and time walking on the bottom bits of his jeans and patching them up again, and time talking to people with cameras on red carpets. And Mummy goes shopping.

And so it was that Mummy and Daddy started auditioning for nannies to find, as Daddy said, 'The very bestest, specialest nanny in the history of nannies, who I will sign to my record label – I mean I will employ to look after Eric.' Sometimes I think grown-ups should pay more attention and remember the difference between real life and make-believe.

Jeeves offered to chip in with helpful critiques while serving the drinks and canapés to the potential hired helps but Daddy said, 'No, thank you, Piers. I should think your opinions are the last thing anybody needs.' He also queried as to whether Jeeves had fallen off any more Segways recently. Jeeves dispensed him a rather cold look and glided out to instruct the kitchen staff as to the exact temperature to heat Sir's milk. The temperature of Mummy was my thought on this. Hmm, I was beginning to get to the bottom of the plastic-tasting milk business. But there was no time to think about it now – the doorbell rang and Jeeves showed in the first candidate.

AMERICA'S GOT NANNIES

So, Daddy and Mummy sat on the sofa next to each other with me on 'Ewick's ickle playmat' between them and waited for the first person to be brought before us. 'Hello,' said a nice lady with brown hair and lots of make-up, 'I'm Bethany and I'm from Beverly Hills.' 'OK, Bethany from Beverly,' said Daddy, obviously thinking this was a rather clever remark, 'tell us about yourself.'

'Well,' said Bethany, playing for time and going pink in the face, 'I'm eighteen years old, and I have always loved babies, and my dream has always been to look after somebody famous's baby, and I think you're amazing.' (Who, me? Or Daddy? Daddy apparently. Humph.) 'And so I would love to look after your baby.'

'Look, love, I'm looking for a nanny, not a stalker,' said Daddy. 'It's a no from me.' Mummy muttered something about me being her baby, too, in case nobody had noticed, and Jeeves showed Bethany out.

Next up was somebody who was so excited to be here that she told us how excited she was to be here roughly every three seconds. She said numerous times that it was like living a dream and that she 'couldn't believe she was really, really here!' and how 'never in her wildest dreams had she thought she would ever actually make it here'. She then started making strange sounds like she had got a fish caught in her throat and I realised she had burst into tears. She was just saying how she was doing it all for her nan when Jeeves quietly ushered her out. 'Well, to say that was dreadful is an understatement,' said Daddy. I couldn't agree more.

Then in came a lady who told Daddy she could make me into a genius. She brought along baby flashcards and proceeded to wave them in front of my disinterested face and say things like, 'Yes, Eric, that's right, look at the picture of Mozart and

Einstein and be inspired.' Then she had a picture with a series of dots on it and numbers next to it. 'Look at the group with just ten dots in it, Eric,' she said, then looked at me and said, 'His eyes are tracking the ten dots, not the twenty dots. He is a very clever boy.' 'Clever Hans, more like,' muttered Piers as he floated around the room, carrying out unknowable and unnecessary tasks. Daddy had a more straightforward critique: 'Are you out of your mind? He's three weeks old!'

Next was a nice lady called Leona, with lots of hair and a smiley face. She said 'Hi' in a shy sort of voice. I liked her. 'Too foxy,' said Mummy straight away. 'I don't know what you mean,' said Daddy. 'I hadn't noticed her looks, just her amazing charisma.' 'Oh, is that what we're calling it these days?' said Mummy. Then she added, in order to make things entirely clear, 'No way! I'm not having her around you a moment longer. Darling.' I thought she meant me, but of course she meant Daddy. So that was the end of Leona. Jeeves showed her out while Daddy followed behind, muttering things like, 'You are amazing. I can make you a star. I can honestly say that was the single best performance I have ever experienced. You've really got what it takes, and I can make all your dreams come true. Er... nanny-wise.' But Mummy had spoken, and it was on to the next one.

Next up was a rather unprepossessing lady with a wedge of frizzy hair and a funny accent. Daddy and Mummy almost told Jeeves to send her away straight off, but she kind of planted her feet and looked like she meant business, and then she was off. 'I can change a nappy in twenty seconds,' she said. And before I knew what was happening she had scooped me off the playmat, whipped off my undergarments, replaced the nappy element with another, and trussed me back up like some sort of infant chicken. It was impressive. Very peculiar but definitely impressive.

Jeeves breezed in and opined, 'Gosh, she's jolly good' to Daddy and Mummy, who were sitting with open mouths and shocked faces. Ant and Dec chose just this moment to enter the fray, and yapped into the room, rolling fur everywhere and barking their little doggy barks. I could have sworn I heard one of them – possibly Ant, or then again maybe it was Dec

– saying, 'You weren't expecting that, were you?' But of course I must have imagined it.

What nobody was expecting was for Jeeves to film the proceedings and then post them on YouTube, whereupon the lady with the brown hair and the funny accent became a worldwide sensation, as everyone found it astonishing that people in Scotland knew how to do things, too.

Next up was a lady called Pamela, who was also a lifeguard and so told Mummy and Daddy that they would always know for sure I was safe any time we were at the beach or I had a bath. She was another one who picked me up off my comfy playmat and dangled me about the place. I wasn't sure if this was entirely for her benefit or if I was meant to be getting something out of it, too. She started singing lullabies to me, so I started waahing, and Daddy quickly informed her that her services would not be required, saying, 'If your lifeguard duties are as good as your nannying, a lot of people will be drowning.'

I took the opportunity afforded by a short lull in proceedings to have a quiet snooze and spend some time thinking about where my next milk might come from, then woke up to hear Daddy saying, 'So, you are the very last candidate of the day. Should we really bother with you?' And a nice man called Will with a big grin said yes, definitely, he was very keen etc. etc. But Daddy said, 'Well, tough, we're not going to!', and sent him packing. Shame, really, as I think he could have been the best of all.

It turns out they made the selection while I was asleep – the cheek of it! I didn't get to have the casting vote about who looked after me? Most unfair, I term it.

So who did they choose? A really nice lady called Sharon. Mummy said she's good because she's too old for Daddy and not foxy enough. Daddy said she's good because she's tough and no-nonsense and will bring me up just right. Jeeves said a lot of things about her that are unprintable, and she returns the favour just perfectly. I think it's going to be really nice having Nanny Sharon and Jeeves around to look after me.

RETAIL THERAPY

Mummy and Daddy went out shopping together today. Well, I say together, what actually happened was this.

I spent the night sleeping like a baby – i.e. waking up every two hours screaming for my mother. (Yes, I know I've done this joke before, but I've also done the routine before, most nights. Mummy says she is getting kind of tired of it, but for me the appeal never wears off) When it came to what grown-ups call morning and what us babies call more of the same – there weren't any difference between night and day in that lovely cave, I can tell you – Mummy yawned several times before crossly yelling to Daddy to kindly sort out some breakfast please as she is breastfeeding again in case he hadn't noticed. I don't think he had noticed btw, as he was holed up in his smoking room with some floaty piano music playing dead loud. Debussy, Jeeves said it was.

So Daddy called back to ask why didn't Mummy ask one of their many employees to bring her breakfast in bed, that was what he paid them for, and Mummy replied that she thought just maybe she was important enough as the mother of his child that for him to get her some sodding breakfast in bed like a real husband, thank you very much. Daddy replied that they weren't married, in case she'd forgotten, but he had promised his undying love for her and wasn't that enough? Mummy replied that she certainly hadn't forgotten and commented, 'If you like it, then you should have put a ring on it.' Daddy rushed out of his smoking room, dropping phones and scissors as he went, which Jeeves effortlessly swooped down and picked up before they had even touched the shagpile, and Daddy announced to Mummy, 'Ooh, I love it when you talk trashy' and they fell to the kissing and smooching again. Yuck.

So then Daddy went to the kitchen and got Jeeves to bring out several trays of croissants and pastries, not to mention coffee and fruit – when do I get to have some of this stuff, I want to know? And Daddy and Mummy fell to scoffing the food and laughing about nothing. When they had finished this particular act of ignoring me, Daddy said, 'I know, what about a bit of retail therapy? Come on, we're going home to England soon where the streets are grey and the shop assistants churlish. Let's enjoy some real luxury in the only country in the world that really knows how to do it properly, the good ol' US of A.' And Mummy said, 'Great idea, darlin', and by the way, what do you mean "home" to England?' Daddy laughed this off unconvincingly, and they got ready to go out.

'Bye, bye, Eric Werick,' said Mummy and gave me a great sloppy kiss on the top of my head. 'Cheerio, little man,' said Daddy. 'Be good, and don't do anything I wouldn't do.' Well, that's OK – from what I hear from Jeeves, Daddy was pretty much out of control when he was little, and there wasn't much he didn't do. Not sure he's changed that much, really.

So, finally they left, and it was just Jeeves and me, Nanny Sharon, Ant and Dec, and the kitchen staff, and the maternity nurses, etc., etc. Jeeves wafted up to me and whispered discreetly, 'How about something completely different now, Sir? Would Sir like to watch the wrestling?' Sir certainly would and Jeeves knew it. Brilliant intuitions that man – he knows what you're thinking before you even know it yourself. So Jeeves switched on the TV, Nanny Sharon walked in, carrying a bucket of popcorn, and Ant and Dec scurried into the room, dressed up in absurd matching costumes. I would like to add that it wasn't until later that I realised the horror extended further – I was also dressed in the same matching costume, and each of us had the words 'I am Simon Cowell's Top Dog' written on our baby/dog gro. Hanging head in shame, or HHIS, as us of the next generation say.

But even that couldn't get me down now. Life was good. Mummy and Daddy, with their sloppy kisses, were out, Jeeves and Nanny Sharon had kicked back, with feet up on the coffee table and beers in hands. Jeeves was explaining in dulcet tones the finer points of four-figure leg locks, Ant and Dec were providing quality weeing entertainment, Nanny Sharon was shouting obscenities and the wrestling was on the telly. Retail therapy, indeed.

All too soon Mummy and Daddy were back. Jeeves instantly switched off the TV, crushed the beer cans with his bare hands and rapidly turned them into designer ashtrays – that man is a quick thinker – and switched on One Direction on the music player. Nanny Sharon quickly fed the remains of the popcorn to Ant and Dec to provide entertaining surprises on Dad's head later on (he sleeps with them on his head. I know, mental). Daddy opened the door shouting, 'We're back!' in case people hadn't noticed. He then instructed Jeeves to 'switch off that racket', and he and Mummy hauled in several palette loads of bags overflowing with clothes and shoes of every shape and hue. Turns out they had gone their separate shopping ways as soon as they reached the outside world, with Mummy patronising the outlets of her favourite designers, while Daddy in turn went to his. But despite this they had both managed to get almost the same clothes – great numbers of blue jeans, Daddy's in extra-long, and T-shirts in various colours that hugged their boobs

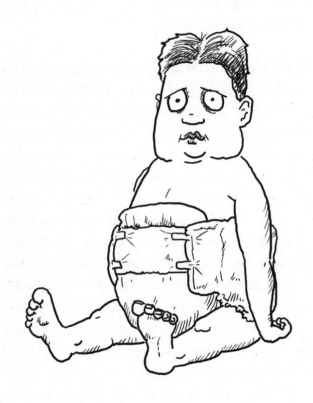

and moobs respectively. Why they bother to spend time and money shopping for clothes when they wear the same outfits every day beats me.

But they weren't content with that. No, they also bought clothes for me too, of course. Because it's a well-known fact of life that babies need to own their weight in clothes to make sure we are never seen in the same outfit twice – unlike Daddy, who is seen in the same outfit every day. And, yes, you guessed it, more matching babygro and doggro outfits in triplicate for me and Ant and Dec. These were, if anything, worse than the previous set. Jeeves's particular favourite was 'I've got the X factor', while my personal nadir was 'I'm worth $25bn' – definitely not trashy at all.

MY FAMILY AND OTHER ANIMALS

Today was a very exciting day – I met the rest of my extended family. I seriously think I am going to run out of space to store in my brain all the mental images, let alone the names of all the many and varied people I have to meet and try to form separate identities for. But a baby must try, I suppose. So today was the day for meeting Mummy's family. There was Mummy's mummy, whose name is Carole but I have to call her Granny America, then Mummy's daddy, who Daddy calls Steven but Mummy tries to get me to call Granpops. Mummy's sister, Nicole, who I have to call Aunty Nicole, and of course my brother – well, half-brother – Adam. I am really not sure what to make of this – I mean, he seems nice enough, all shiny white teeth, baseball caps and strung-out American vowels, but do I really want someone else vying for Mum's attention? Hashtag #siblingrivalry, you know what I'm sayin'.

But, then again, it's not really much of a competition, is it? I mean, I am a super cute baby, everyone says so, and that just doesn't compare to an eight-year-old, now does it? OK, fair enough, you can hold a conversation with him, which you can't really do with me yet. You can play a game of catch with him, which I admit I'm still not entirely up to speed with, and you can even rely on him not to cry uncontrollably at the slightest provocation. Actually I doubt you can depend on that – not with anyone in this family. I found Daddy sobbing the other day after he discovered a tiny black speck on one of his white T-shirts. Literally sobbing, he was. Jeeves had to comfort him with a new one straight from the packet. Pitiful I call it.

But, to return to the subject of kid vs baby, who wins, I was beginning to think maybe an eight-year-old does have the upper hand over me after all. And Mummy seems awfully keen on him – it's almost

like she loves him nearly as much as she loves me!
How dare she? What to do?

Of course Jeeves provided the answer – he had the
idea that I might actually like my brother if I gave
him a chance. So, he had Adam come over and make
funny faces at me – and I must say, they were a little
cartoonish, somewhat on the clownish side. I mean,
a little more obvious than a real abstruse Marcel
Marceau master would have been going for, but it's
true, they were funny. There's something about kids
– they are seriously good entertainment for babies!
I'm not exactly sure why. Maybe it's partly because
they are a bit more our size, rather than absurdly
large compared to us, like grown ups are, and they
don't have overly big hair like Harry, or overly
painted lips like Mummy. They don't obsess about
clothes or looking just right, and they don't care
about making themselves look silly. And they don't
toss their hair in a very foolish manner when they
laugh (naming no names, well, OK, I mean Daddy)
and they like to squoosh you all about and roll their
heads in your tummy and don't worry they're going
to break you. They're just, well, normal, I guess.

Yes, all in all, do you know what – as Daddy would say – I'm a fan. Maybe this is why in some countries older children bring up younger children – it's more fun and everyone is on the same wavelength. Seems to me like it makes much more sense rather than having twenty-seven adults each competing to look after one baby, to wit, me. But, hey, who am I to argue with Simon Cowell? No one argues with him, do they? Although perhaps I will when I'm just a little older...

HAVE PASSPORT, WILL TRAVEL

Mummy and Daddy went to get me a special little book with a photo of me in it today. It was all very complicated. First, there was the process of getting just the right photo of me. As if there aren't enough photos of me already! But, no, we needed more, and in this one I had to have my eyes open, but wasn't allowed to smile in case my teeth showed. Jeeves tried informing the passport people that I don't have any teeth so there's very little danger of them showing, but it was a thankless task. But eyes open, mouth closed, well, I tell you – it's trickier than it sounds. Basically it was achieved by Jeeves making a series of funny, but not too funny, faces at me while Daddy played Peepo behind a cushion.

Sorry, I've got to digress slightly to tell you about my love of Peepo.

God, I love the game of Peepo. It literally is the funnest thing ever! Daddy ducks down behind cushion, where the heck has Daddy gone? Will I ever see him again? Daddy reappears in front of cushion. Wow, he's back! Surely that's not going to happen again in my lifetime? And then it does happen again, straight away too. Awesome! I don't think I will ever tire of it.

Daddy got tired of it, but luckily the photo was in the can by then – well, in the camera but you know what I mean.

Then, once the photo had been achieved, Daddy and Mummy had to fill out lots of forms and get people to sign the forms and Daddy kept saying, 'We still don't have a plan for who is going to witness the photo of Eric. It has to be a professional person.' And Mummy said, 'Let's ask Louis', because I think she likes Louis, but don't let Daddy hear me say that. And Daddy said, 'We can't ask Louis – he's not a professional!' And then Mummy suggested

Harry Bighair but Daddy gave the same answer even more vehemently, and so on. Finally someone remembered Jeeves, who had momentarily suffered a coughing fit, and Daddy agreed that he was definitely a professional something; he just couldn't say what, but in any event the problem was solved.

The upshot was that I then had a passport, which meant that I could travel abroad to somewhere called England, or 'home' as Daddy calls it. What's going on with this endless series of homes? I'm just getting used to one and I have to become accustomed to another. Jeeves says it's playing havoc with his ability to blend, chameleon-like, with his surroundings and glide noiselessly from one room to another. Not sure why he's quite so keen on doing that, but everybody needs to have a hobby, I suppose.

So, what does having a passport mean? It means more air travel on the Syco private jet, bought from all the money he makes from telling people they can't sing – oh God, no! – or, as Jeeves calls it, the Psycho private jet. But it also meant that in the preparations for this momentous journey to 'home' to see another Granny (Granny England this time), and human Ant and Dec and 'Cheryl' and all of my other 'aunts' and 'uncles', I began to understand certain things. I know why when Mummy feeds me when we are out of the house the milk has a plastic taste – she puts milk into bottles. And then Daddy feeds me from those bottles, presumably because his T-shirts are so tight that they stop his moobs from becoming proper boobs. What a swizz.

But what I have also found out is that sometimes it isn't Mummy's milk in the bottles: it is 'baby formula' – double swizz! And today, when I started some experimental exercising with the things on the end of my arms, which seem like they might be useful for sticking in my mouth, I discovered why I had been feeling so very content, that last half hour. As I tried to delve in I inadvertently grabbed hold of a small blue plastic thing, which had been in my mouth, and then let it drop to the floor. I had had a dummy in my mouth, all this time! Now *I* sure feel like the dummy. Talk about swizz-ville! I mentioned to Jeeves that I was appalled at this underhand behaviour by my parents and he replied, 'They mess you up, your Mum and Dad, they don't mean to but they do', which he said was poetry. Doesn't sound like poetry to me – I mean, it doesn't rhyme or sound pretty or anything. But as Jeeves said to me, I could no more define poetry than a terrier could define a rat. He's deep, that man. Really deep.

As well as finding out about my lying, cheating parents with their dummy-pretending-to-be-Mummy, and their formula-pretending-to-be-milk, I chanced upon another discovery. Daddy had spent most of the morning in his smoking room. Smoking, presumably. The sweet tones of tinkly piano (Mozart, Jeeves said) and serenading violins (Tchaikovsky, apparently) were emerging from time to time, when they weren't being hastily switched off by Daddy every time 'So Macho' rang out and he had to talk to someone on the telephone. Then Daddy emerged, looking particularly pleased with himself, and brought out some things out to show me. But just at that moment Harry Bighair arrived with three (or was it four?) of his friends, and Jeeves showed them in. Daddy quickly shoved whatever he had been carrying behind one of those faithful cushions, and started putting loud jangly music on the players and talking too loudly to Harry Bighair and smiling with his too-white teeth.

I gurgled amusingly at Harry Bighair and his friends for a few minutes in the hope that they would go away. When that didn't work I thought crying might achieve the desired result more quickly, and it did. Jeeves rapidly showed them out again and Daddy poured himself 'a stiff G and T'. Jeeves, ever the unruffled, reached behind the cushion and proffered the offending objects to Daddy with the words, 'Here you are, Sir's Sir. Would now be the right moment for Sir to have this?' Daddy quickly grabbed them from him and said, 'Yes, thank you, Piers, that will be all', and motioned him away. Daddy checked that Mummy was still fully occupied mooching by the pool talking to assorted members of her Silverman clan – and she was. And then Daddy picked me up and said, 'Now, Eric, I have something here for you, which is very special.'

He picked up each of my feet – not the dreaded piggy rhyme again, please! But no, it wasn't. This time he squeezed and squished my feet until they each fitted into a small, embroidered blue bootee. For all of several seconds. Until I kicked them off. Whereupon Daddy went through the whole procedure again, saying things like, 'Now, just wait a moment until I have it on properly before you start flailing around. Wait, wait… there!' He sat back and admired his handiwork. 'Yes, they are really beautiful. Perfectly proportioned.' (Yes, my feet are perfect, thank you!) 'And, if I say it myself, expertly stitched.' Expertly stitched?! Why would he care? And suddenly the penny dropped – OMG! Daddy wasn't just proud that he had managed to squish the bootees onto my unwilling feet, he was proud because he had made the bootees! And now I saw the truth behind Pecial Blankie.

'So, Eric,' said Daddy, 'this is just between you and me.' And Jeeves, I thought! 'Here are your own Cowell bootees, just like the pair which were made for me, matching your own Birth Blanket, which is all hand-sewn by me, with your own name stitched in here, see?' I saw alright. I saw that the 'smoking room' was one major pretence. And I saw why whenever Daddy was around there was always a pair of scissors and classical music not far away. But seeing clearly wasn't enough. I had to listen, too. Specifically listen to Daddy talking about the virtues of blanket stitch versus running stitch, and the pros and cons of hand stitching over machine sewing. I had to listen to endless details about needle sizes and thread thicknesses. He said that one day he was going to show me his thimble collection.

Like I say... OMG! My Dad, Simon Cowell, a keen male seamstress! Who knew? To summarise... ROTFL!

Although you'll have to do the rolling bit for me. I'm working up to it.

HOME, JEEVES

So today we flew 'home' to England to Daddy's house in London where we are going to live. Except when we're living at one of Daddy's other houses in America. And except when we're living in Mummy's apartment in New York so that Adam can come to stay. And except, I should think, when we have to stay in a posh hotel somewhere else for some other reason. I have a substantial amount of growing up to do and I would appreciate a bit of peace and quiet in order to get round to doing it, if it's all the same to everybody else. What is it the child experts say – normality and stability, that's what children need? But is anyone here listening? Are they, hell.

The first challenge was packing all the mountains of stuff we planned to take to our 'home', which is presumably fully furnished with quite a lot of stuff already – how much stuff can two adults and a baby reasonably use? We were flying by Daddy's private jet. Jeeves says the trains in England are no good. So perhaps I can make lots of money by telling the people who run the trains that they can't run trains? Jeeves says that's not one of my best ideas but I think he's just annoyed because no one else has had that idea yet; it's all mine.

Daddy says flying by private jet is the only way to go. Mummy agrees. Jeeves says it's just as well because if we tried to take all that luggage on Ryanair it would cost about as much as a private jet. Nanny Sharon said, 'Come on, let's get this ******* show on the road, and get the haul the hell out of here before the ******* pilot gets drunk!' I don't know why Nanny Sharon always speaks in stars; I think it's something to do with ratings.

Luckily I managed to sleep through a lot of the packing palaver, and the endless saying goodbye to people palaver, so there was just the flying nightmare palaver, and then the unpacking palaver to look forward to. When we got to the airport, with all of its ghastly noise and wind tunnels, there were loads more people wanting to say goodbye to us. They kept shouting Daddy's name and taking photos – obviously. Of course they were hugely interested in me too, but did they really love me for me I mused, or just because I am Daddy's son? Fortunately this unpleasant moment of mortal introspection passed and I decided to just lie back and suck my dummy after all. Dummy – swizz! I'm still cross about that.

While Mummy and Daddy sat on chairs and pretended to enjoy a pleasant conversation over the combined noise of me, and the engines, screaming, Jeeves hovered around, saying things like 'There, there', while Nanny Sharon dangled me around the place, shouting things like, 'That's right, Eric! Let it all out! My children all enjoyed a good scream from time to time. My husband still does.'

Eventually time passed and we landed. 'Back in Blighty!' said Daddy. 'Yesss,' said Mummy, some-what less enthusiastically. And sure enough out of the plane we got, into England, and boy was it cold! Maybe there was a method in some of their shopping madness after all. Many layers were stuffed onto me, Pecial Blankie was pulled extra-specially high up by Daddy (!) and the hazardous journey to a waiting car commenced. We made it! And after some clever buggy folding from Jeeves and some car seat shoving and clipping from Nanny Sharon, with the accompanying speaking in stars, of course, we were in said waiting car and heading 'home'.

Daddy's house in London is OK, I suppose. I mean, it's big and there's lots more plasma screens and telephones and big white sofas, of course, but it's not next to a beach like Mummy's family's house, and there aren't any nice lizard things in the garden, which Jeeves says are geckos, so I don't think that much of it. But Daddy seems to think it's rather great, so I didn't hurt his feelings by sharing mine. Nanny Sharon said it was '******* brilliant' and 'much better than that tramp Lady Gaga's pad'. Jeeves, of course, is the man to rely on in such circs. He merely queried whether 'To settle Sir into his new surroundings, would Sir like a little glass of something about now?' Daddy thought Jeeves was asking him the question, but was disabused of this opinion when I demurely accepted Jeeves's invitation, and was only mildly disappointed to find out he meant milk rather than whisky and soda.

Of course there were lots more people to meet at the house, and all of them wanted to take a photo or seven of me, preferably with their own heads shoved next to mine during the process – 'selfies', they called them. Why don't you sod off and take a picture of someone elsie, I prefer to call them. As there was sadly little I could do to prevent this cavalcade of amateur photographers, I decided to consent graciously and only get up a bit of waahing action when the whole thing really started dragging.

Then Daddy told me all of the other people I was going to meet: Granny England (who is Daddy's mummy), Uncle Nicholas, who is Daddy's brother with the same mummy (Granny England) and Daddy (Eric the Great), Uncle Tony, Uncle Michael, Uncle John and Aunty June, who are Daddy's half-brothers because they had the same Mummy (Granny England again) but a different Daddy (not spoken of or named). They all seem to have lots of children, but many of them aren't children any more, meaning I have lots of cousins of varying ages who I will also have to meet and try to learn their names. I hope you've been keeping up, because I for one am very confused. 'Team Cowell' Dad calls us all – well, I guess even I can handle that one.

But that's not the end of the list, oh no. Then there's Aunty Sinitta, Auntie Nicole, Uncle Gary, Uncle Dermot, Uncle David, and so on and so on. But apparently none of that lot are real aunties or uncles. And then there is Cheryl, and she's not even called Auntie. Jeeves says it's because Daddy is cross that she's more famous than him. But I don't think that can be true – Daddy says he is more famous than the Pope and the Queen, and I think he should know.

LITTLE ENGLAND

I met Granny today! Granny England that is, who is very different from Granny America – she is really nice! She likes to pick me up and say things like, 'Oh, you've got your Daddy's nose', which is obviously not true, in any possible way. And when I goo goo at her she says things like, 'You're much less of a handful than your Daddy was when he was a little baby!' but then she hasn't seen a full meltdown yet. I tend to reserve those for when there are assembled crowds of photographers in order to get best exposure, or for the baby torture of flying – have I communicated to you how very, very much I hate flying?

After a quantity of dangling on Granny England's part, and accompanying grizzling on my part, it was agreed that Daddy, Granny and I would go out to 'see London'. This time I was to have a new form of transport: being strapped to Daddy's chest in a baby pouch. Dad told me that baby slings were designed by ancient civilisations so that the baby could be rocked by the natural movements of their mum and dad, and always be near their heartbeat to soothe them, blah, blah, blah, and also because, more importantly, any time baby wanted a drop of milk, it was near to hand. Provided baby is strapped onto Mum's chest, of course – I was not so lucky! All I had was Dad's hairy chest for company. And if it was milk I was after from that environment I could clearly whistle for it. Not that I can whistle, obviously.

So, anyway, after the usual endless fussing and checking whether there were at least twenty-three bibs in the changing bag and fourteen bottles of milk etc., etc., we set off. Just me and Daddy and Granny. And Jeeves. Oh, and Nanny Sharon. They followed behind with the changing bag, and the buggy, and a playmat, and Ridiculous Knitted and Overly Cute, and Pecial Blankie, of course. Mummy sensibly stayed behind to read a book.

Wow – the houses in England are so little! There is nothing more than about four floors high! And the cars are tiny, too, but they move much faster than the cars in America. I don't know what that is all about but it seems very peculiar to me. Why would you bother having huge cars that can go zillions of miles per hour and then drive them incredibly slowly and cautiously, like they do in America? The little cars that you have here which zip all over the place seem to make a lot more sense. My favourites are the tiny electric cars. But Daddy says they are 'just for liberal leftie whining Greenies', whatever that means.

And the roads are tiny, too! This means it's actually possible to walk to places on the pavements without people thinking you are an utter loony, like they do in America. Jeeves says if you are caught not driving somewhere in America but trying to walk there instead, you are likely to get arrested for causing a public nuisance. Nanny Sharon says it's 'total ******* madness and no wonder everyone's fatter than a ******* Sumo wrester in ******* America.' Jeeves was more restrained, of course – he merely opined that it is a public health concern of a highly significant proportion which threatens to divide humanity from its inalienable connection to Mother Nature. No, I don't know what he means either.

Not that we did much walking, of course; it was mostly an experiment as to how quickly can you jump in and out of taxis with a baby strapped to your chest, and how short a distance can you walk with a baby strapped to your chest without feeling the need to take the weight off and hop into another taxi.

First stop, Big Ben, because Granny England wanted me to have a look at it – not very big is it? I mean, it's a jolly old clock and everything, but apart from that, what does it really have to offer? Then Daddy showed me Hyde Park Corner and he and Granny stood squinting at the statue of the Angel of Mercy and her horses in silent wonderment. That is to say, along with all the other tourists, we stood looking around us at the passing traffic, wondering what the heck all the fuss was about. Jeeves later told me that the statue of Boudicca is much better and began expounding on the history of Boudicca, first Queen of England, and how she made a stand against the Roman invaders. Interesting stuff, that. Whereas what we were doing was hanging with all the other people who had trekked halfway across London or even halfway across the world in order to stand on a glorified roundabout and gawp up at something they didn't have a clue about. But I didn't want to spoil Granny and Daddy's fun and they seemed to be happy enough playing at tourists in their own city, so I kept my views to myself, which is in no way due to the fact that I still haven't quite mastered the whole talking thing yet.

Next up – the London Eye. Sounds cool, doesn't it? Actually it's just a fairground wheel. Is that really the most spectacular thing anyone in London can think of? With the number of people there waiting to go round on it you would certainly think so. Luckily, we weren't among them. Jeeves tells me London is a city with a fascinating history that goes back over 2,000 years and while we are strolling along by the river, my face plunged into Dad's hairy chest, Jeeves gently lulls me to sleep with talk of Roman walls, and hidden war rooms, and sublime ecclesiastical flights of architectural fancy such as St Paul's. But I am whisked away from this reverie by Dad and Granny's sudden desire to 'see what's really cool in

London, what everyone who's anyone really wants to see – the shops! Like Harrods and Selfridges'. Shops? Sorry, but really? A bunch of places where you can buy more stuff you don't need?

And btw, I found out during the next gruelling two-hour tour of the shop that Selfridges doesn't even sell fridges. When I grow up, I'm going to open a shop called Sellphones and it won't sell phones, not even cell phones.

MOTHER'S DAY!

**(Or as we call it in our house,
Another Simon Cowell Day)**

So I woke up today, bright and cheerful as always. Well, I mean, I woke up screaming uncontrollably and wailing most piteously for some milk and a cuddle. Momentarily Jeeves was at my side providing both, which all in all rather restored one's faith in humanity. A change of nappy and a change of clothes later and I was deemed presentable enough to be brought into the marital (non-marital) bed to a fanfare of trumpets – for it was Mother's Day!

I do mean a fanfare of actual trumpets, btw. I mean, this is the Cowell household, you know. Yes, Dad had hired a group of actual trumpeters and there they stood, lined up against the wardrobe in Mum

76

and Dad's bedroom, trumpeting away to their little hearts' content. Mummy was sitting up in bed in her best dressing gown with floaty number underneath, and Dad was wearing his pyjamas (actually a Spiderman onesie LOLz! – but don't tell anyone) and smiling a luminous smile of white iridescence. Yup, he's had his teeth painted again. Jeeves held me in his arms and we all waited for the loud trumpet music to stop. Well, the others waited, I had no such compunction – I found the noise frankly rather trying, extremely loud and staccato as it was, and so I started out with a small grizzle, which I was anticipating bringing up to a crescendo of waah.

So Dad quickly stopped short the proceedings: 'OK, OK, I've heard enough. That sounded like a ship sinking. Your performance was like an audition for *One Flew Over the Cuckoo's Nest*. This is not what I bought when I heard you in rehearsal in the US. This was a perfect example of how a performer can go from amazing to awful. I'm sending you home, and I'll pay for the flight.' The trumpeters shuffled out, muttering things like, 'Charmless nerk', 'I've heard he's Mr Nasty, but that really takes the biscuit' and 'Yes, indeed he will pay for our flight; that was actually in the contract!' And 'At least I got a quick photo of his Spiderman onesie and I'm going to put it on Twitter. That should wipe the shiny smile off his big Syco face.'

So after Mum had calmed Dad down with soothing noises and insincere comments like, 'It was a lovely gesture, darlin'. I know you meant well, even if it did end up producing a nasty feeling all round and Eric screaming.' Then she called to Jeeves to bring me over, and finally I was back where I should be, at the very centre of all attention. 'Oh, ickle darling Eric,' she cooed, accompanied by a lot more unmitigated idiocy, but I put up with the baby talk as at long last in return I got cuddled and dandled and all that stuff. Dad took down the top bit of his Spiderman onesie, made a lunge for me and put me back on his chest, his hairy, hairy chest. Ah my, the things a baby has to put up with. 'And now,' shouted Dad, at a sudden alarming volume that made me do a major startle reflex, 'let breakfast begin!' Good job we babies have these startle reflexes, you know, otherwise all those thousands of years ago when we had to fend for ourselves in the jungle we could have been easy prey for a variety of wild and savage beasts. But, good old startle reflex – always there to keep us safe…

In this particular instance it didn't entirely work, as immediately in walked Nanny Sharon, loudly blaspheming and carrying trays of delicious smelling bacon, sausages and other goodies. Now, this is *so* not fair! Everyone knows that I am on a strict diet, which is even stricter than all of Mummy's and Daddy's bonkers fad diets – breakfast of hot water with lemon, papaya juice with lime, spinach smoothies, no wheat, no gluten, God forbid any carbohydrates, only green foods on Wednesdays, blue foods on Fridays and nothing at all Tuesdays and Saturdays, etc., etc. (I bet they all pig out like Ken Clarke would when presented with a slap-up feed of sausages and mash on Sundays, but they don't tell anyone.) But my diet is purely milk. Not even a drop of water am I allowed. And yet here they were, flaunting their fried breakfasts in front of me as if I didn't have a sense of smell, or a sense of injustice.

Well, it all went pear-shaped anyway. Daddy looked his proudest at having remembered Mother's Day and then having got the staff to produce a Mother's

Day breakfast to end all Mother's Day breakfasts, while Mum looked quietly shocked. When Dad could take this silent anger no more, he timidly raised the query of what exactly it was that might be wrong. Mum said, 'If you don't know, I don't know why I should take my time to tell you.' Dad replied, 'Please, sweetheart, you will have to tell me what it is, because indeed it is true that I don't know.' Mum pulled her dressing gown tightly around her and folded her arms in a swift cross motion saying, 'You know full well I am trying to get my figure back, and I can't be eating a great big bloated breakfast like you English people think is healthy and do that at the same time now can I, for goodness gosh sake?' Dad replied, 'But, sweetie, first of all you look gorgeous anyway, and secondly, while you are still breastfeeding you can really eat what you like – you need to be eating for two. That is meant to be one of the benefits, no?' 'Yes,' said Mum, 'but I can't eat like a pig, can I? Oh, you don't understand!'

And then she turned away and looked like she was going to waah, too. Luckily, Jeeves was there to save the day. 'Would Sir's Sir care to give M'Lady the card from Eric?' 'Thanks, Piers!' Dad trilled merrily, and grabbed a small blue piece of paper from Jeeves's outstretched hand upon which had been inexpertly daubed 'Happy Mother's Day, You are the best Mummy Ever! Love from Eric Werick'. Oh God, he's actually put Eric Werick in writing – honestly, you just can't get the parents these days, can you?

Mum was suitably mollified and said things like, 'Oh Si, darlin', you are the best, sweetest man in the world. No one knows you like I do (apart from Sinitta, and about a million other people, I thought), and no one knows your wonderfully kind, sweet, good nature. Oh thank you, my darlin' cupcake.' (Cupcake?!) Said Dad, 'Don't thank me, thank Eric, the card is from him, you know.' And then they both fell about laughing as if this was the world's funniest lie.

Nanny Sharon and Jeeves retired gracefully to watch the World Darts Championships and cheer loudly. Their work here was done.

I CAN'T SING

I found out today that Daddy has decided he is not quite famous enough at the moment, so he is paying for a musical to be on in the West End of London all about him. It is going to be called *I Can't Sing*, which is very accurate because he can't. It's been written by Uncle Harry, the man with the very big shirt collars – I wonder what's wrong with his neck that he needs such big shirt collars to cover it up?

Anyway, tonight was going to be the opening night and Daddy and Mummy were both going along and they were going to meet lots of Daddy's friends like Uncle Harry, Uncle Louis, Aunty Amanda, Uncle David, Aunty Myleene and Aunty Sinitta. Although not Cheryl because she is 'recording in a music studio today', i.e. is cross with Daddy for having this brilliant wheeze for making himself even more famous than he already is. And she's also cross that the person in the show playing her just says, 'Why aye, man' all the time.

So Daddy got out his best patched-up-at-the-bottom jeans, and his favourite T-shirt, which is the same as all his other T-shirts. Jeeves shined Daddy's pointy shoes, and he put on a new black overcoat, which is the same as his old black overcoat. Then Mummy complained that Daddy was wearing the same old (by which she meant new) T-shirt that he always wears and couldn't he for once make an effort and wear a shirt? So Daddy said that choosing his clothes was his business and he wasn't going to let anyone boss him around, and why did Mummy think he hadn't ever got married? Did she think it was because no one would have him? Because she was very, very wrong if she thought that. There was Sinitta for one, there was Mezhgan, not to mention Joanne Davidson, whose dad was a painter, and had been really keen on him at school. Mummy replied that she wasn't trying to be the boss of him, she just wanted her 'lil Simey Monster' to look as gorgeous to everyone else as he was to her. (I thought she said little Slimey Monster, but Jeeves assures me she didn't.) Well, she won him over with that. He changed into a shirt alright. But she's definitely not the boss of him, oh no.

Mummy wasn't quite so quick to get ready, though. First she tried on all the new clothes that she and Daddy had bought in America. Then she tried on all the new clothes that she and Daddy bought in Selfridges (I'm still cross they don't sell fridges). Then she said things like, 'Darn it, nothing looks right today!' And Daddy said things like, 'Darling, you look lovely whatever you wear,' but when she tried on a white furry hat and said, 'Does Mummy look pretty?' he did himself no favours at all by replying, 'I don't mean to be rude, but... to be honest, love, you look like a poodle.' Mummy started speaking in asterisks, just like Nanny Sharon, and going an unusual shade of purple. Daddy put his arm around Mummy and said, 'You're emotional, darling, and I understand. It's a big night out for us all, because there is going to be a wonderful, wonderful show, and it's all about ME!'

Then Mummy pulled a silver disc off the wall and threw it at Daddy's head but Daddy avoided being garroted, which had clearly been Mum's intention, and instead caught it brilliantly. Nanny Sharon zoomed in to rescue the situation and said, 'Now, now, everyone, let's calm the hell down', but that seemed to make Mummy even more cross and she started shouting, 'Nobody cares about me and what I'm like. It's all just Simon Cowell this, Simon Cowell that, you're so *amazing*, Simon Cowell! What about me? And what about Eric? Are we going to leave him at home again?'

Glad somebody had finally mentioned my name in all of this. About time, too. Of course, it took Jeeves to come up with a plan. That man has a mind like a razor. For his first trick, he picked out Mummy's old favourite dress from one of the wardrobes and said, 'It suits M'Lady down to the ground.' Mummy simpered and went off to put it on, and came back in looking mollified and happy. Daddy said how wonderful she looked in it, etc., etc., and Nanny Sharon sat down to do Mummy's make-up, despite Mummy's voluble protestations.

Then Jeeves suggested that there would be so many real celebrities there at the opening night that nobody would notice him. And so he could slip into the theatre carrying me in my car seat and then I could sit with Daddy and Mummy and we could all enjoy nice family time, while watching a West End blockbuster all about Daddy, which Daddy had paid for – because that's what families do, don't they?

After a few more hours kerfuffle while Mummy tried on about seventy-six pairs of shoes until she found the ones which 'showed her dress off to perfection' (Jeeves's words, of course), we were finally ready to leave.

And so I had my first taste of a red carpet. It didn't taste too good I can tell you – all thready and dirty. I'm joking, of course; Jeeves didn't let me get down and have a good play on it and lick it, much as I would have liked to. Instead he whisked me inside while Daddy and Mummy were having their photos taken – well, Daddy was having *his* photo taken and Mummy was photobombing. Good job Daddy had got his teeth painted again a few days before, as he was doing a lot of smiling for a lot of cameras. I mean to ask him if his face gets tired, when I can work up the words.

There were lots and lots of people all around, and everybody was either holding a phone or a camera to take a picture, or looking into a camera or a phone that was taking a picture. Some people were doing both at the same time. I'm not sure what everyone does with all these photos afterwards. Where do they all go to, I wonder? Does anyone ever actually look at them all? Perhaps all the photos get together when nobody's looking and have big photo parties and then take photos of themselves and put those photos on Facebook for other photos to look at and be jealous of.

Anyway, while Daddy was talking and smiling and Mummy was simpering and trying to get anyone to listen to her instead, and while Uncle Harry and Aunty Amanda and all the rest of them were saying loud hellos to each other and making fake kissing motions, Jeeves and I slipped inside when no one was looking.

And boy, was I glad he smuggled me in. Partly because the inside of a theatre is really cool and I was going to get to see real people up on stage, not just people on the telly – don't matter how big your plasma screen is, it's still just a screen, and that ain't nothing like the real thing. Or at least that's what Grandad in America had said to me when he was talking about how life used to be better in the old days. But also, I was glad to be here because it seemed like there was scope for serious mischief – what I mean is, having a good old baby meltdown just at the wrong moment.

In Jeeves's capable hands the car seat seemed comfy and cosy and it wasn't too long before I fell into a woozy state of dreaming about milk. Ah, milk. Suddenly I was rudely interrupted by some majorly loud noises coming from the stage and all hell broke loose in my head. Wow, live entertainment gets you every which way, doesn't it? It was noisy, there were bright lights flashing, people around me were gasping and laughing in equal measure and loads of people were dancing and singing from the stage. Blimey.

I don't know if it was good or bad, I'm really not qualified to judge, but it certainly was intense. And there was a man who looked just like Daddy on stage! But no one who looked like Mummy – well, except for Mummy, who was sitting next to me, constantly looking anxiously at me and saying things like, 'Please don't have a meltdown now, Eric. *Please*!' Of course I had been planning exactly that, but unfortunately I discovered that the noise everywhere else was so loud that when I started up a small waah no one heard it except Mummy. And then she gave me some milk in a bottle (swizz), and that shut me up. I had another go at bringing attention away from the stage and back to me once the milk was finished, but unfortunately Jeeves then produced a dummy from his waistcoat pocket and that did it for me. I don't get it – I know it's a con – I am fully aware that it doesn't produce any milk, and it isn't even nice soft Mummy's hand. It is a small piece of blue plastic. And yet, and yet – I like it. It really is comforting and friendly to suck on. Does disrupt the normal growth of my teeth, though, and delays the onset of talking, but what's that to me?

So the rest of the show passed off without incident from me, sadly. I have to confess that with Jeeves's rocking arms and the Dummy of Doom I was as quiet as mice, i.e. I made small scrabbling noises and occasional squeaks. But luckily, other forces were at work, called 'Things often go wrong in live events, which is in no small measure why we invented television'. And things did go a bit squiffy on stage, but at the end of the show Mummy and Daddy clapped and cheered and then stood up to clap and cheer more loudly, and so the rest of the audience thought they should, too.

Daddy announced to various waiting parasites – sorry, members of the profession of journalism – that it was his second baby of the year. How very dare he, suggesting that parade of nonsense was remotely equivalent to the miracle that is me! Huh. I shall have words with him about this one day, I can tell you. Unless I work out which side my bread is buttered on, that is. Not that I eat bread yet, but you know what I mean.

Finally we got to go home, and Daddy said, 'Well, that was a triumph and worth every penny!' and

Mummy said, 'Great, now your ego is going to be literally the size of a planet.' Jeeves said nothing and Nanny Sharon just said, '****'.

COMEDY OF ERRORS

Today was a quiet day chez Cowell, by which I mean only about fifty-six people came round to the house. In theory they wanted to tell Daddy how fantastic his show was; in practice they wanted to show off to their friends that they knew the great Simon Cowell well enough to go round his gaffe, as long as they brought a congratulatory bunch of flowers or bottle of booze, that is. And of course they wanted to see ME! Some of Daddy's bestest friends (I've lost count of how many people I've overheard saying, 'Well, of course I'm a really good friend of Simon') still hadn't actually met me yet. Can you believe it? What a scandal!

So today I finally got to meet Ant and Dec. I mean

the real Ant and Dec, not their furry namesakes. They were some of the fixty-six who came round to the house – they brought both flowers *and* bottles of booze, just to make sure they were let in, I think. Jeeves had organised a sweepstake to see if anyone could successfully tell them apart for the entire duration of their visit. The prize was to be the bottles of booze they had brought – quite nice stuff too, according to Jeeves.

Well, things started off quite badly, as Jeeves got them the wrong way round the moment he let them in through the door. 'Hello, Sir Ant,' he oiled, only to be informed by Sir Ant that he was, in fact, Sir Dec, like. 'Apologies, Lord Deck,' he opined, and was then dealt with in what I considered a rather rough manner by Sir Dec, who brushed him to one side while spouting, 'For God's sake, I am a national treasure, like! Can no one do me the decency of noticing that I look bloody nothing like the other one and get my sodding name right?'

Well, apparently no one can, because then in walked Mum. 'Hello, Declan, darlin'!' she breezed. 'No one calls me Declan except my own mother,' said

Lord Dec between gritted teeth. Luckily just then, Jeeves recovered himself, stopped sniggering into a cushion, and thought fit to rescue the situation. 'Would the Sirs care for a drink?' he questioned, addressing them both as one. As one they replied in the affirmative, and just then Dad emerged from his 'smoking room'. But he had left his labours in a bit of a rush, having heard all the commotion, and being sensitive to the possibility of impending disaster in the form of two short arses getting major-league cross with everybody (and Jeeves has reliably informed me that they fight like well-trained Mexican dwarf wrestlers), he naturally wished to avert such a crisis. Soooo... in his rush he had brought out with him his latest sewing creation! Arghhhh!!

It was quite nice, actually – a name cushion for me, inscribed thus: 'Eri'. Well, it's short and sweet, you can't argue with that. But people should know that Dad was making it for me, crafting it with his own hands! I can see the tabloid headings now: 'Cowell's got talent – but not in a good way', or 'Music media mogul makes a mess of material', or possibly 'Simon Cowell likes to do a bit of sewing in his spare time – who'd have thunk it?' Jeeves says I'm not very good at making up newspaper headlines, and I should stick to my day job, of lying around and waving my arms and legs. I regarded that remark as slightly uncalled for, and made a mental note of a frowny face against the man.

But, gem of a chap that he is, Jeeves almost immediately made up for his cruel honesty with a genius remark to all and sundry that really saved the day: 'Ah, Sir's Sir (that still cracks me up), so that's where the cushion for Eric, which his grandmother has nearly finished, has got to. Excellent! May I place it in the dining room to await her next visit?' Dad muttered something along the lines of 'Yes, jolly good, thanks, Piers. Run along now, won't you', and then smiled a super-dazzling white smile, which with the matching super-white T-shirt rather blinded everyone – both literally, and to the actual turn of events. It's a clever trick if you can pull it off, and my Dad can – that and his top. And so in a single leap, he was free – disaster averted, for today at least...

So then, Dad and Mum and Ant and Diddy Dec, as Nanny Sharon calls them, sat down to congratulate each other on being so famous and successful. I find this kind of conversation pretty tedious, hearing it quite a lot as I do, so I decided it was time for a bit of baby attention. Now, I don't like to pull rank too often, and create the baby equivalent of the blinding smile that forcefully draws attention away from everything else that is going on. But every now and then, why not? I mean, it's a baby's right, isn't it? So, I decided to go for it. I thought of waahing, but that's a bit old hat these days, and anyway now I know that Jeeves has a permanent supply of super-comforting blue dummies (swizz swizz), waahing won't get me anywhere apart from one of those. No, I had a different idea today.

Well, obviously I did start off with a little bit of waahing – I am a baby after all – but not too much. Just enough so that Mum and Dad would think I'd like a bit of holding and jiggling, but not too much, so that they would think the Tiny Twins could step in and do a bit of baby dandling. Right on schedule, Ant, or possibly Dec, said, 'Ahh, is little Eric Berick – excuse me, what? – getting a bit restless, like? Would he like to join in the conversation and have a bit of cuddle time? Can I pick him up, like?' he asked Daddy, as if Daddy was in charge of me. I think you'll find that's Mummy actually. Or thinking about it, possibly Jeeves. Anyway, Dad duly looked at Mum, and Mum said, 'Sure, AntandDec (good idea of Mum's, that). Eric has a very sweet nature, he won't mind you picking him up at all. He's a super-precious darlin' one, aren't you, Ericissimo?' (What? Just what?)

So, I was handed over to AntandDec, who held me rather inexpertly, betraying his fear that he might suddenly break me with an overshow of confidence, and said to me, 'Ahh, yes, that's better, like, isn't it, little Ericky? Yes, you ickle, ickle man.' Right. Now is the time, I said to myself. And so just when he had manoeuvred me so that I was precisely over his nice new suit, I let rip. Yup, I pooed all over him. Hahahaha! Smiley face! LOLz! You should have seen their faces, all of them!

'Oh Gosh, I'm so sorry! He's never done that before. Oh, good grief, it's come right out of the nappy and through the babygrow and everything!' said Mummy. 'Oh dear me – your suit, I'm so sorry!' 'Ah, no, it doesn't matter, really, like,' said AntandDec, meaning OMG this is horrible, it really does matter, very much indeed. 'Oh no, it's awful! You must let us have it dry cleaned, really!' 'No, no, honestly it's fine, I'll just, er, like, well er, like er…'

And so while they were all jibbering like idiots, as if they'd never seen a bit of poo before, as if they don't wipe their own bottoms every day, in swept Jeeves and Nanny Sharon to sort things out. 'Here, Sir,' said Jeeves to Dec, or possibly Ant, 'let me escort you to the bathroom, where you can change into one of Sir Simon's suits which he had as a child. I think it will fit you perfectly.' And meanwhile Nanny Sharon swooped me up and took me off for 'a nice new set of clothes', while quietly congratulating me on the way for such mastery of event and timing, and mildly chastising the staff for openly laughing and posting their photographs on Instagram.

So, once I had emerged all clean and forgiven (yeah, yeah, soz buckets, and all that), I found that AntandDec had gone. Nobody won the sweepstake, which meant that Jeeves got to keep the booze; I realise this was his cunning plan all along. I went to sleep that night and slept the sleep of the just. A fine day was had by all; well, especially by me. Yes, it had been a fine day to be alive and be a baby. With a self-satisfied grin on my face and a manufactured blue plastic dummy in my mouth (swizz) I fell asleep.

Btw, I have decided to call the real Ant and Dec Squiddly and Diddly. But if all this gets too confusing just say, and I will have the editor shot. Daddy says I can.

LITTLE BRITAIN

I met a new friend of Daddy's today, he is called David and he is very, very funny. He makes really funny faces that make even Jeeves laugh, and that man is normally implacable, I can tell you. Daddy laughs, too, but he pretends not to. Mummy smiles with what Jeeves calls a wry smile, but doesn't laugh; Jeeves says this is because Americans don't have a sense of humour. David picked me up and told me stories about dentists and things; didn't mean much to me as I don't have any teeth, which I think people could bother to remember when they're telling me anecdotes about their latest successful novels, but I can see he meant well. Then he gave Mummy and Daddy the present he had brought for me – a door bouncer! Now this is seriously wowzer!

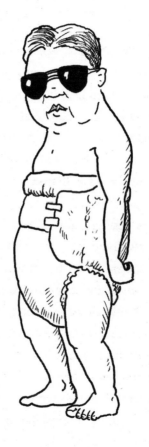

Mummy said, 'Thanks, Dave, honey, we'll keep that in a really safe place.' But Daddy said 'It's OK, darling, this will be great for Eric! Let's put it up and see if he likes it.' Mummy replied, muttering under her breath, 'No, Si, I'm not having him bouncing up and down from a doorway like a crazy person. No way.' To which Daddy replied, 'Oh come on, let's give it a try, he might really like it', to which Mummy said, 'No…' But luckily while they weren't looking Jeeves had already attached it to the nearest doorframe and Nanny Sharon popped me in.

Wow, it was cool! Finally, a bit of independence! I still haven't worked out how adults manage to use the things they call legs to get about on, but inside the baby bouncer I managed to use the things inside the Cowell Cutie Bootees to bang on the floor and make myself bounce upwards. I mean, epic! Mum was still muttering about it not being appropriate, but I think it is totes approbe. They get to have their fun in the private jet and big cars, so why shouldn't I have mine? Then Nanny Sharon ramped it up a stage further.

She brought something she called a mirror and set

it up against the wall opposite so that I could see – another baby! This one also had regulation Cowell Cutie Bootees, and a babygro like mine, proclaiming: 'Simon says… relax!' (obviously I can't read, so the fact that the other baby's top had backwards mirror writing on it, and it actually said xaler … syas nomiS is irrelevant to me – OK, smartarse? To return to the plot…). And it was looking right at me. Now that's what I'm talking about! Oh yeah, finally a friend my own size for me to play with and have bouncing competitions. I thought this was so funny that a strange gurgle came out of my mouth and Daddy and Mummy both said, 'Oh listen, his first laugh!' Well, nothing's just ever been that funny before, do you see? Jeeves says I won't have this much fun again until I'm old enough to go to Thorpe Park, whatever that is.

Jeeves busied around rustling up smoked salmon canapés and torn hazelnut almond brioche amuse-bouches for Mummy and Daddy and David to eat, and they all stood in the hallway eating and laughing, and grinning like idiots and watching me go up and down, up and down and laughing at the other baby. Like I said, that David is quality – the man knows how to make everyone laugh, me included.

Of course Nanny Sharon knows what's what, and so after a good bit of bouncing she took me out (meany) and off for a bit of 'quiet time' while Daddy and Mummy celebrated my first laugh with a bottle of Krug, which inevitably led to the kissing and the hugging. David muttered something about having to swim to Norway and hastily beat a retreat, and Jeeves effortlessly disentangled the baby bouncer from the doorway, ready for another day.

Baby bouncing sure does give you an appetite – so it was time for a good lot of milk for me, courtesy of Nanny Sharon via formula and bottles (swizz, swizz), and then a nice lie down. When I woke up later I found that Mummy had gone out to do some more shopping because she'd discovered she had one pair of shoes that she had worn more than once, and Daddy came in to spend some quality time with me. Of course what this really means is a chance for Daddy to do some of the things he can't do when Mummy is around because she Disapproves.

So, he got the kitchen staff to make his favourite food. 'Hey, Geneviève,' he called to the chef, 'no more of that torn brioche idiocy, bring me out some real food, won't you?' So Geneviève lovingly prepared fish fingers, baked beans on toast, followed by Angel Delight for pudding. 'Hey there, Eric, it won't be too long before you're able to get your gnashers on this good stuff, you know. Once you've got any gnashers, of course,' he told me cheerily. Always with the teeth conversations, these adults. Then he switched on one of the big tellies and started playing a DVD he keeps in his handy manbag for easy accessibility, and the TV started showing some fast-changing brightly coloured moving pictures of people and dinosaurs, and cars with stones for wheels. He started singing out, 'Flintstones, meet the Flintstones, they're the modern stone-age family!' Well, I wouldn't really call it singing... As Granny England whispered to me the other day, 'Btw, your Daddy has a dreadful voice. And he can't dance.'

But the joy of singing can be in the ear of the singer, and so several episodes of *The Flintstones*, several fish fingers and an Angel Delight later, Daddy was in a very happy mood. He turned to me reflectively; it was clearly time for a Daddy discourse. Uh-uh, here we go...

'You know, Eric,' he started up, 'when you are truly immersed in an activity, you reach a state of heightened awareness of that activity, and corresponding subjugation of all alternative pursuits and distractions.' Uh-uh, I thought, I think I'm with you so far, although not entirely sure why you are mentioning this. Could it be we are about to be treated to a dissertation on... the joy of sewing?

'You see, Eric, through such focus you can enter a truly metaphysical state of oneness with your soul, your identity, your being (right... and the punchline is...). And so it is with sewing.' (Yup, I knew it!) When I choose chain stitch over feather stitch, it is a choice based on reason, but also founded in emotion. I feel that choice deep within my heart and then I act upon it. I cut the thread with the scissors and that cut is that of a tribesman cutting his own skin to mix his blood with his brother's. Then I join the needle and the thread and they become as a single sacred unit, tied together with a knot that seals their fate. Lastly I pierce the material with the needle, and with each tug of it as it pulls the thread, causing the fabric to be at the same time both distorted and made anew, I feel the blessing of creation upon me. It is truly an experience that goes beyond the mortal. It is an epiphany. It is divine.'

Right. OK, Dad. All I can say to that is … LOLOLOL!!

'Oh, and by the way, Eric,' continued Dad, 'there's no such thing as Father Christmas and you'd better get used to it.'

Thanks, Dad. I've no idea why people call him Mr Nasty.

A ROOM WITH A VIEW

I discovered today that one of the many people who have been round to the house recently, a rather extravagant chap with long hair and high cheekbones by the name of Laurence Aberystwyth-Bowen, rather than being one of the regular hangers-on actually does something to earn his money. Specifically, he does designing things. I don't spend much time in my bedroom here at 'home', because I'm either in Mummy and Daddy's bed (which I call Mummy's bed), or I'm being paraded around various rooms of the house when guests arrive for them to goo-goo over me, and for me to poo over them. (It's a fair exchange and I'm happy with it.) The only times I'm really in my bedroom are when Nanny Sharon takes me off there to let me have some 'quiet time'

– which I call 'screaming time' – or when Jeeves and I want to kick back and have a bit of quality Jeeves and Sir time, waving arms and legs and staring at the ceiling. He's almost as good at it as me.

But whenever I am in my room I notice a few things about it – it's big. I mean, really, really big. You may think it's a long way down the road to the chemist's but that's just peanuts to my room. Oh no, that's space. Yes, sorry, that was something David was telling me about and I got a bit confused. Anyway, it is big, my room. Not as big as space obviously, and not in fact as big as most of the other rooms in the house, but the point is, it is big compared to me.

As are most things, it has to be said, apart from Squiddly and Diddly, of course. Both sets of them. But it also looks big because it's white: white walls, white ceiling, white door, white curtains. You'd begin to wonder if I would suffer from sensory deprivation in here, if it wasn't for the fortunate presence of various Pooh Bear characters projected onto the ceiling by means of a very clever baby-soothing device which doesn't involve a piece of plastic being shoved into my mouth whenever it looks like I might be about to recite a Shakespeare sonnet. Of course it doesn't work as effectively as a soothing device as the aforementioned piece of plastic, but hey, you can't have everything.

Anyway, so Mummy told me the other day that the all-white thing had been her idea, and she had got the Polish builders in one day when Daddy wasn't looking and had them take down the Sinitta posters, the Susan Boyle wallpaper and Olly Murs curtains that Daddy had put up and replace them all with the calming presence of white. As she said, 'White is the perfect colour; for it is all colours, in perfect balance and harmony. It is the colour of the awakened Spirit; the light of perfection; the light of the Cosmic Consciousness, the Divine Light.' Good grief, Americans don't half talk rubbish.

Well, Dad had a bit of a rant about it when he got home, saying things like, 'There's nothing wrong with Susan Boyle wallpaper – Chris Hoy has it in his room' and 'What do you mean you threw my Sinitta posters in the bin?' and 'How the hell do you think we are going to get puke and poo stains out of that pure white carpet?' Some of which I agreed with him on. But it was clear from Mum's face – sternly set and determined, like Brian Blessed on the Atkins diet turning down a cream cake – that the white was staying. Also, she picked up a pair of Dad's favourite jeans and made a rather unpleasant gesture with a pair of scissors. So Dad manned up and got with the programme. Well, I *say* he manned up, he retreated to a corner to have a small cry and go through the textile recycling bag to cut out some Olly Murs likenesses to save for keeps, but all in all he was reasonably grown-up about it.

But it seemed that everything was going to be different for my own special room at *The X Factor* studios. And that was why Laurence Aberystwyth-Bowen had been at the house. He had finished the design and the builders and wallpaper putter-uppers had done their bit, and today was the day when I was going to see what he had created. Yes, it was Dad and his lad time – with accompanying Jeeves, Nanny Sharon and Laurence, of course – and we all took the trek from west London to north-west London (they're like different planets, I tell you) to see my new room in the studio.

We arrived at the studio with Dad rather flustered because he had forgotten to pack the extra reserve pack of baby wipes, and because Nanny Sharon had leaned out of the car on several occasions during the journey to shout at taxi drivers, cyclists, pedestrians, other motorists, police officers, traffic lights, bollards... Jeeves, of course, was entirely unflappable – calm and quiet throughout. Turns out he has micro near-invisible in-ear headphones and was listening to the Arsenal match throughout the entire journey. However, being a man of impeccable taste and decency he saw no need to force his sporting opinions on anyone else and made no comments on the game at all, either to us or online. He did punch the air on one occasion but managed to turn the act into that of swatting a fly. He's such a respectful man, and so refined. I think I want to be Jeeves when I grow up.

Dad was very excited to show Jeeves and Nanny Sharon the studio, although they both said they had seen it before and, to be honest, knew it pretty well. Dad paid no attention to this and showed it all to them anyway. I was pretty uninterested, I have to say – I mean, was there milk involved? Was it all about me? If not, that's my interest pretty much gone.

Finally Laurence took us to where the real action was – my room. And all I can say is, OMG OMG, OMG, OMG!!!

For starters, it was most definitely not white. But it wasn't because there were any pictures of Olly or Susan or Sinitta on the walls, I'll give you that. No, there were pictures of someone different altogether. My dad! Yup, you wouldn't believe it, but it's true. Eye-poppingly huge blown-up pictures of Dad all over the walls, the ceiling, even the rug! Dad wearing sunglasses, Dad wearing jeans and a white T-shirt, Dad smiling with the world's whitest teeth, Dad looking pensive, Dad looking happy, Dad obviously having just said something he thought was extremely witty. Yes, all those my-dads were there. Looking into the camera, looking at me. Looking dead humble, oh yes.

Nanny Sharon nearly exploded and said things like, 'You can't do this to a child, it will scar him for life! You utter **** *****! Is your ego so large that it is literally the only man-made object that can be seen from space? My God, you are living proof that money obviously doesn't buy you style!' Jeeves, even Jeeves, was somewhat rocked by the vision before him. He managed to scrape out, 'Is Sir's Sir entirely certain that he is fully cognisant of the effects that intimate exposure to such, how can I put it, inappropriate images, can have on an infant's brain?' before excusing himself temporarily and sneakily posting a photo on Twitter accompanied by the hashtag #cowellgonecrackers. Laurence, however, calmly intoned that 'Being a dad is the new black and everyone had better get used to it. Like the seventh cavalry emerging o'er the brink of a hill, I give you – Simon Cowell at large!' They sure were large, he was right on that.

Dad looked at the pictures of himself. Jeeves muttered sotto voce that it was like being in an *Alan Partridge* set. Nanny Sharon tried to restrain herself from taking to the wallpaper and ripping it down with her bare nails. Laurence waited with bated breath. And Dad said ... 'Do you know what? I think it's really, really good. If I'm being honest, I think this is absolutely fantastic. This has the X factor. I knew

Britain had talent, but I didn't know it had this much talent. It's not just a yes from me, it's an always.'

Lorenzo smiled and I took the opportunity to let out an unworldly waah that not even Jeeves's endless supply of dummies could silence. I wanted home and I wanted Mum. Now!

'Home, Jeeves, and don't spare the horses!' I cried, in the only way I knew how. And it worked. Thirty minutes later we were home.

I resolved never to go to *The X Factor* studios if I could help it. The trouble is that I'm not sure I can help it, what with being entirely beholden to all the adults in my life for everything in my life.

Jeeves and Nanny Sharon told Mum about the incident and next day, when Dad wasn't looking, she got the Polish builders to go and sort it out, and she cut off the head of one of my cuddly horses and put it in Dad's side of the bed in case he got any ideas about switching it back. A brutal tactic, but it worked. I never saw Laurence Aberystwyth-Bowen at the house again.

I'm beginning to think Mum might be right about white.

PRETTY IN PINK

Today was the best! Jeeves was exchanging my nappy for a later model while whistling, 'I'm leaning on a lamppost at the corner of the street in case a certain little lady comes by' – he says it is not autobiographical – when Dad came in and said, 'Hurry up, Piers, David will be here in a minute!' (Good news! David is so funny, he is definitely my favourite uncle.) And, Piers, don't forget to put the pink outfit on Eric.' What? Now, I don't know much, but I do know that I never wear pink. For some reason it's just not a colour that I'm allowed.

But today was different, so Jeeves, while sighing subtly at the absurdities of life, picked up the pink tights and squeezed and fed my legs into them. Then a pink flowery skirt, a bright pink T-shirt which said on it 'Race of my Life', and a pink cardigan with a feather edging (boy, was that tickly), which Jeeves, after much swearing under his breath, finally managed to get me into. What the heck was all this about? I mean, I know Mum and Dad like me to be all dressed up every day for no very good reason that I can work out, but this was all different. What was it for?

Well, all changed and fed, and ready to face the day despite wearing pink, I was carried into one of the sitting rooms in Jeeves's strong arms and placed in Mum's lap for a few minutes of adoring time. 'Ah, Eric, you ickle ickle, darlin' etc., etc., etc., while Dad's phone rang out 'So macho! So macho!' until he answered it. 'Yes, David, we're all here. Yes, Eric's all ready.' Ready for what?

Soon the doorbell rang. Jeeves let David in and after the usual pleasantries – 'How are you?' 'Still immensely wealthy, thank you. And you?' 'Yes, also still immensely wealthy, thank you' – Dad said, 'So, are you sure you're on for the challenge?' David said that he certainly was, so long as I was up for it. At this he looked at Mummy, and Mummy said, 'Well, I think as long as we make sure he's fed and changed first and he seems really settled, then it will be OK.' Jeeves made soothing noises in the background to the effect that he would ensure I was fed, changed and 'settled'. Mum seemed happy with this, and Dad said, 'In that case, let's get going.' WHERE? I wanted to know. What in the world was going on?

Jeeves showed David to a guest room for him to change his clothes and when he emerged some time later, well, all I can say is … WOW! Like me he was also dressed from head to toe in bright pink! Pink wig, pink T-shirt, pink skirt that stuck out at right angles (Jeeves said it's called a tutu), pink tights, pink trainers, pink lipstick and pink boingy things on top of his head – 'deely boppers', apparently! He looked like an enormous giant fairy! Mum and Dad laughed uproariously, and even Jeeves couldn't stifle a snigger. This was clearly the reaction David was after because he grinned a huge grin and then swiped me off Mum's lap and said, 'Now we're Little and Large. How do we look?' 'Terrific!' beamed Mum and Dad together. (This is obviously something they share, a so-called sense of humour. I had been wondering what it was they liked about each other, other than a taste in clothes. And money.)

Jeeves leaned in to me and whispered that this was all about something called charity. This happens when a society cares about something, but doesn't care enough to vote in a government that will actually give enough money to the cause. So instead people have to go around jumping out of aeroplanes wearing only their underpants, and hitch-hiking while carrying a small washing machine in order to persuade normal people like you and me to part with our hard-earned cash to sponsor them to raise money for the thing. And David is quite an expert at it, by the sounds of it, with his speciality being swimming. Oh God! I wasn't going to have to dunk myself in the freezing-cold waters of the river in London, was I? Surely, Mum wouldn't agree to that? I mean, after the *X Factor* room I know my Dad is bonkers, but Mum is relatively sane, isn't she? Isn't she?

Luckily, just as I was considering getting all worked up about this hypothetical event, Jeeves intervened.

He coughed discreetly to raise attention and when everyone turned to meet his gaze he queried whether those present would perchance like to take a glance at the buggy. When Dad said, 'Sure thing, Piers!' Jeeves glided from the room and returned with my lovely buggy unbelievably dolled up – pink ribbons on the side, pink tinsel round the top and pink feathers on the handle. 'Way to pimp Eric's ride!' said David. Mum snorted in horror, and Dad said, 'Do you know what – I don't mean to be rude but, that looks like something dreamt up by Mickey Mouse on helium.' (See, I told you he likes that phrase.) 'If I'm being honest, that is not Manchester United, that is Dagenham. Butlins, yes, Simon Cowell's son, no.' But David said, 'I love it, it's perfect! Well done, Piers!'

And so I found out that David was going to raise money for breast cancer research by pushing me in my new pinkified buggy while running 5k around a famous park in London called Hide Park. That sounded great! Did it mean that we could have fun games of hide and seek? Nope. What it meant was that Jeeves was going to have to try and keep up with David – no easy task, apparently – in order to have a constant supply of *pink* dummies to hand. Nanny Sharon, Mummy and Daddy were going to be cheering me on (I mean, cheering David on) and at the end, Dad said, I was to meet someone pretty special.

Well, they were clearly very happy about it, but honestly, the things a baby has to do these days! Isn't it enough that I sit around and wave my arms and legs, drink milk and poo all over celebrities? That used to be good enough for Frank Sinatra and Marie Curie when they were little, but no, I have to be some kind of constant accessory to fame and fortune. Put out on show as if I have no feelings of my own, no concept of my own identity. Now, of course, I support charity as much as the next baby, and this one is definitely very worthy, but does the raising of money for it have to involve the belittling of me? Hardly seems fair or necessary. But, well, I guess it could be fun at least.

OMG, it was! So much fun! After the usual three-hour palaver of leaving the house involving lost dummies and missing baby wipes, etc., we finally got moving and reached Hide Park, and started the next three-hour palaver of leaving the car. At last, mission accomplished! By which I mean we arrived at the starting line.

IT'S FUN TO RUN

There were thousands of people there! Even more than the number of people who visit my house on a regular basis, and I didn't know there were more people than that in the world! Most of them were got up in a sea of pink, like Uncle David and me – Jeeves said we looked like a vast flurry of urban flamingos. Were we, like them, about to fly? Or were we about to dunk our heads upside down in lake water and eat the fish that made our skins pink? Sometimes I think Jeeves goes too far in trying to educate me. I know he wants me to rise above my birth and escape the social prison I have been born into, but is it essential I become a marine biologist before my first birthday? I think not.

But it was not the time to have an extended conversation with him on the subject, partly because I still hadn't really mastered how to make much more in the way of noises than waah, and partly because – woah! – the race had started! There was a cacophony of noise as thousands of pink, blue and turquoise trainers hit the tarmac, and thousands of pairs of stretch Lycra leggings stretched just a leetle beyond their comfort zone. We were off! David loped along with his giant legs making giant strides, and his deely boppers going twenty to the dozen, and, much more importantly, I was also zooming along! It was so great! Why don't Mum and Dad take me running in the buggy? It's so much fun! I was all safe inside it, with straps and cushions and all of that, but I was being jiggled around in a very pleasing fashion. I saw another Mum running along with her buggy and her baby and she and David smiled a big smile to each other. And then David overtook her, of course – did I mention David is the best uncle ever? He's totes my BFF, that's what I say!

Occasionally I caught a glimpse of Jeeves – he had gone for a more traditional approach to running attire – tweed plus fours, a starched white shirt, brown hunting jacket and a tie. Standards, that's what the man has. Constant poise and standards. Unfortunately, neither would have served him very well in a 5k run through Hide Park. (Btw, Jeeves says I'm spelling it wrong, but I've told him that spelling is the fascism of the ruling elite and I refuse to kowtow to it. Well, to be honest, I didn't say that exactly. I actually just let out a bit of a fart instead, but I think my point was well made nevertheless.) So that's why Jeeves concluded running wasn't the clever way to do things. Yup, he brought a scooter. Not a silly kid's scooter, like some of the small, pink-clad things some people were trundling along upon, but a man-sized racing machine of a thing. He glided along on two wheels, retaining almost complete mastery of it while at the same time proffering pink dummies in my direction.

But David was having none of the proffered dummies – he waved Jeeves away with a panting, 'Not now, Piers, you cheating *******', and I continued to have no need of dummies, permanently jiggled as I was being, with all my senses assailed by the fresh air, the sound of pounding feet and the thrill of the chase.

At one point I heard a loud string of expletives and looked up to see Nanny Sharon cheering us on from the sidelines. David raised up his hand that wasn't attached to my buggy with a safety strap and punched the air. 'Good on you, David!' called out Nanny Sharon. 'Right back at you!' called back David. And on we zoomed. Past Joan of Arc, past Wonder Woman, past some very hot-looking Teletubbies, past several very tall bananas, and way past an entire colony of comedy penguins.

I spotted Mum and Dad, each wearing oversized sunglasses and white T-shirts – Dad in his trademark overlong jeans; happily Mum sees no need to follow this particular fashion 'trend'. They were waving frantically – Mum was clearly indicating that she thought David was pushing the buggy too fast, and she was in fear of something dreadful happening. Dad, however, thought it possible that we wouldn't win, and so was urging David to go faster. Both called out, 'Hi, Eric', and thankfully managed not to disgrace themselves in public by adding the suffix Werick, instead calling out, 'See you at the finish line.' 'Make sure you're there first,' added Dad.

But David paid no attention: 'Don't you worry, Eric, it's not the winning that counts, it's the dressing up like women!'

And sure enough, of course, we didn't win. Dad tried to pretend he didn't mind, Mum was so delighted to see me again in one piece that she didn't notice what anyone else said or did but just picked me up and said, 'My God, I must be mad to be hanging out with this bunch.' Then she apologised to God for taking his name in vain before getting back to the business of cuddling me and generally being delighted with life. David looked like he had hardly broken sweat, and Jeeves looked like, well, Jeeves, but on a day out.

It was all pretty fabby, but then it got even fabbier. To a chorus of thousands of pink-clad runners and their supporters suddenly bursting into screams of excitement, in walked a lady with very nice hair and unnaturally bright lips (because she's worth it, apparently), and Dad said, 'Hi, Cheryl, come and meet Eric.'

BECAUSE I'M WORTH IT

So this was the famous Cheryl Cole? Well she seems nice enough. She came towards me with her long hair flapping in the wind and after some kisses with Mum and Dad and a bit of gentle banter between them, which Dad either won or pretended he had won, the subject turned, quite rightly, back to me. Mummy asked Cheryl if she would like to hold me, and Cheryl of course decided that she would. Well, I should think so, too! So Cheryl swooped in on me and picked me up and I waited in anticipation for a stream of the usual baby rubbish.

But good grief, this was quite different – it *was* a stream of the most unconscionable rubbish, but in an entirely new way. It sounded rather like this:

'Why aye, man, now whuse the moost gorgeus lukin baba this siede of the Otlontic, eh?' I didn't have the faintest idea what she was talking about and looking at Jeeves and Mummy, I could see that they were also struggling to comprehend. Daddy has clearly mastered the art of deciphering this peculiar lingo because he smiled knowingly. Jeeves, of course, hid his total lack of comprehension under the veil of an exceptionally blank stare, and appeared to find something in the middle distance that required concentrated investigation. But Mummy wasn't so circumspect. She turned to Daddy: 'What on earth is Cheryl talking about, darlin', you'll have to translate for me!' Daddy sighed. 'Oh dear, Cheryl, it's never going to work with Americans, you know.' Cheryl replied, 'Why aye, man, I dinna ken what th' problem is all aboot', and I thought her accent had slipped rather to somewhere north of the border, but Jeeves says that's a common problem when people try to do regional accents, so I thought I wouldn't mention it.

Cheryl was about to launch into another burst of 'Why aye, man', followed by a further stream of incomprehensible gobbledygook when I manage to stop her short with a brilliant wheeze. I have been secretly practising moving my lips together to see if I can engineer some of the sounds that the grown-ups manage to seemingly effortlessly produce – I mean, talking. Well, I can't say that I got much closer to actual words, but what I was able to do was... blow a great big raspberry! Wow, it was fun! Partly the raspberry itself – very satisfying, I think I shall definitely add this to my list of favourite things to do – but most of all the reaction.

Cheryl was visibly appalled and began to hand me straight back to Mum (another brilliant result of my dastardly plan). Mum looked slightly embarrassed and began making apologies for me, but Dad loved it. 'That's my boy! Do you know what, Eric? You have genius comic timing! I can honestly say you are the funniest baby in England.'

I was pretty proud of myself, I have to say; even Jeeves couldn't suppress a snigger. And it means I have another weapon in my baby arsenal of things I can embarrass adults with, alongside the tried-and-trusted ones of waahing inconveniently loudly, and pooing over A-listers. But little did I know, Cheryl had an ace up her sleeve, or more accurately, a rose on her bottom. Yup, if you spend any time with Cheryl Cole you will find that anytime the attention becomes diverted away from her and her extremely bouncy hair (did I mention that she's worth it?), she has the killer blow to end all killer blows. Something that stops conversation stone dead even more rapidly than a burst of the old 'why aye' stuff. Without so much as an 'Eric, do you want to see my etchings?' she had unwrapped her wrap-around dress to reveal the bikini under-neath (like a good Girl Scout, she's always prepared) and growing around it in the bum area was a massive, and I mean *massive*, tattoo of roses. OMGGG!!!

Seriously, that must have hurt like hell when she had it done. What in the name of all that is unholy is that going to look like when she's sixty? It's not as if it looks good now either. It looks mental! But it sure is impressive, I'll give it that. Mum's jaw hit the floor and Jeeves suddenly found something extremely diverting on his shoe, but Dad hardly batted an eyelid. 'Yeah, I've seen it all before, Cheryl. Come on, love, put it away!' Cheryl tossed her long shiny hair, laughed and re-wrapped her dress. I've got to say, my Dad is a pretty cool customer – being so nonchalant in the face of an entire rose-painted bum. I tried to join him and attempted to muster up another raspberry to show the world that I'm more important than anybody's bum, even one with a picture of the goddamn Mona Lisa herself on it, but I just didn't have the bottle. All the fight had gone out of me. I just had to face facts – that bum is genuinely more attention-grabbing than me. No fair! And apparently her sister has a son she's called Keric. Talk about deliberately trying to sideline me – making it look like my name is one consonant short of what it should be. When it isn't – mine is the normal name, goddamit! You couldn't make it up, which is why I haven't.

There was only one thing for it – scream loudly and beg for Mum to take me away. Both Mum and Jeeves saw my plan, and Jeeves ushered Mum away from the scene of the fray before the waahing got to an embarrassing volume, and chaperoned me back into a normal, sensible world where people didn't paint their bums and try to upstage babies. Dad made his excuses and joined us, and to receding calls of 'Why aye, man!' we made our way to the waiting car and home. What a day! Blimey, the things I do for charity!

A RIGHT ROYAL MESS

I woke up today to find that things were not quite their usual blend of calm as exuded by the various kitchen staff, coupled with various bouts of frenetic baby pandering and socialising from the parents. I wasn't sure what was up, but something certainly was. Even in Jeeves, the embodiment of calm nonchalance, I observed a slight perturbation; he was continually smoothing down his hair just so with his right hand. A tiny nervous habit. No one would have noticed it but me of course, but I know the fellow so well now that even a slight movement out of place and I can tell something is disturbing the chap's renowned unruffled and measured approach to the iniquities of life. As I say, something was up.

But what was it? Soon Dad emerged from his 'smoking' room (or, as we know it should be called, his 'sewing' room) with a soppy grin on his face and a small blue top in his hand. 'Well, it's all made, and right on time,' he announced proudly. I was settling down to a nice cuddle with Jeeves but Dad soon put a stop to that. He manhandled me from Jeeves, saying, 'Thanks, Piers, I will get Eric dressed today. I'm a real hands-on Dad, you know,' and off we went to my room for several minutes of squashing and squeezing me into Dad's new creation. It was a blue T-shirt upon which he had carefully hand-stitched the name ERIC in appliqué. Oooh, there's posh. It was actually quite nice, I have to say.

He emerged with me suitably personalised, after only a minimum of waahs (when my right arm became hopelessly trapped within the folds of the material and it looked like it would never make it through the armhole), and proudly showed me off to the assembled crowd, i.e. Jeeves, Mum and Nanny Sharon. I saw Geneviève peeking round a pillar, too and of course Ant and Dec were running around everyone's toes, vying for attention but not getting any.

Everyone was suitably polite about Dad's handiwork, and said encouraging things like, 'You could sell those at Camden Market, you know' and 'It's a yes from me' from Jeeves. Dad gave him a withering look. 'Do you know what?' said Dad, 'I think it's really, really good.' 'Yes, darlin',' agreed Mum, 'it really is.' Dad sensed that no one else thought the thing was quite so impressive as he did. 'Oh, you're all just jealous,' he said pouting, and left me in Jeeves's arms to go off and get himself ready.

That was when I found out what we were getting ready for. Nanny Sharon told me we were going to see Prince! He's an old rock star, it seems, and he made things called records (don't ask me what they are; I'm post iTunes generation, I'll have you know) a long time ago, which Nanny Sharon just loves. They're not her husband's favourite ('He loves Dido,' she said, 'but don't tell anyone. It doesn't fit his rock'n'roll image.'), but she can't get enough of purple rain and starfish and coffee. Well, it sounded like a bit of fun.

Meanwhile, as Nanny Sharon was filling me in on the plan for the day – why grown-ups insist on telling me the plan for the day when I can't think beyond where my next meal is coming from, I have no idea – Mummy was getting herself ready. She was in even more of a flap than usual about it all so she did the normal routine of trying on about a billion outfits and then going for an old favourite (maybe start with the old favourites next time? Just sayin'…). I don't quite know why she's so bothered – we're just meeting some old rock star after all, just the artist formerly known as the artist formerly known as Prince. Dad, as usual, had no such bother choosing his apparel: he decided it wasn't a blue jeans and white T-shirt day and therefore it must be a black suit and white shirt day. Simples.

I must say, there's a lot to be said for having a man's approach to clothing. Maybe women should try it one day.

Finally everyone was ready, and with a cry of 'To the Cowell-mobile!' from Dad, we were off. Well, I don't know if I've told you, but I have a rather quixotic relationship with cars (no, I don't know what that means either). I mean cars are great, aren't they? They take you from one place to another and they rarely complain. They shelter you from wind, rain and sun, and you can listen to music in them (Dad usually has Classic FM on in his car). They come in lots of different colours, though Dad's is always black, boo hiss. You can give them names: Nanny Sharon calls ours Betty. And… they are just super for sending you off to sleep. It's like clockwork – within a few minutes of being in the car I'm off to the land of nod, usually joined by Dad, whose head starts nodding pretty quickly, and I've even seen Jeeves's eyelids close for a little longer than normal. But they do sometimes go round corners at a bit of a lurch I've noticed, and, well, to be frank, that can play havoc with a baby's digestion. And so it was today.

I was busy processing the milk which Jeeves had given me before we set off, and was having rather nice baby dreams about great big lakes of milk that babies can drink from at will, without having adults say when it is, and is not, 'time' for milk when suddenly the car reeled a little more to one side than I was expecting. Ridiculous Knitted Elephant did nothing to help, and I found it impossible to prevent myself from spitting out a reasonable quantity of the aforementioned milk, and of course it went all over

Dad's latest handiwork. Well, I think it would be fair to say that Dad did not react calmly.

'Oh my God! This is a total disaster! Oh, Jesus, what are we going to do?' Dad shrieked in horror. 'Stop the car! Stop the car!' The car was stopped and Mum proceeded to unwrap me from the lovingly made creation I was wearing, which had now become somewhat milky and vile, while making soothing noises to Dad – 'Don't worry, darlin', it's OK, it's really not the end of the world.' Dad struggled to hold back the tears, but it was all too much for him and he began weeping uncontrollably over the sodden blue top, clutching it to his manly breast and sobbing into its dairy-soaked folds. However, he was forgetting we had Jeeves in the car: Jeeves who can always be relied upon to solve any crisis, no matter how apocalyptic.

He coughed discreetly to gain attention. 'Yes, Piers?' said Dad, peering up through tear-stained hands. 'I think,' intoned Jeeves gently, 'if Sir's Sir will recall, in the "I'm a Hands-on Dad" bag, Sir's Sir packed another hand-made top which might perchance well suffice to take the place of the somewhat moist one currently in his hands.' 'Yes, but Piers,' said Dad, his voice rising to a crescendo of genuine freak-out proportions, 'that one is not finished!' He scrabbled frantically in his baby bag, through wipes and dummies and Overly Cute Dogs, and pulled out another beautifully crafted appliquéd baby T-shirt, which simply said on it 'ric'. Dad hadn't got round to doing the E yet. 'He can't wear that,' cried Dad in a heartbroken howl. 'It's not his name. We'll be a laughing stock!'

'Ah,' said Jeeves, 'but we could say it is his nickname for short. And the r isn't in capitals because you are so, how can I put it, down with the kids, Sir?'

'Brilliant, Piers!' said Dad, a small ray of hope shining in his eyes. 'Do you know what? I think that might just work.'

So I was pushed and squeezed into the new blue top, announcing to all the world that my name was 'ric'. And once again neither Ridiculous Knitted nor Overly Cute did anything to help. The things a baby has to put up with for the sake of his parents' pride, honestly. HHIS. (Hang head in shame, in case you don't know...)

So, off the car rolled again, and once more the soporific effects of the motion were set in place, and soon Dad and I were dreaming of puppies and milk respectively, and then the kerfuffle of doors opening and closing started and I woke up to find that we had arrived. So where did this guy Prince live?

Well, Buckingham Palace it wasn't. But Kensington Palace it was!

And that's when I discovered that I hadn't completely understood what Nanny Sharon was talking about – her fault entirely, I'm sure – and that she hadn't meant the ageing rockstar called Prince but an actual Prince! Two to be precise, baby Prince George, and his Dad, Prince William, as well as his Mum, Princess Kate.

OMG, even I have to admit I was quite excited. I mean, music media mogul celebrity cash and fame is one thing. But actual royalty, well, that's another.

Mummy and Daddy were very well-behaved, I have to say! There was less of the hair tossing than normal from Mummy and a lot less of the 'I'm the most important person in the world' swagger from Daddy. And Nanny Sharon hardly swore at all. Jeeves was, well, Jeeves – you can't improve on perfection. And I was still where it mattered, absolutely at the centre of attention. Or was I?

FIRST AMONG EQUALS

We were shown into this quite enormous room with almost floor-to-ceiling windows, draped in vast, heavy velvet curtains, and filled with very plush-looking real vintage furniture that really didn't look like it came from Ikea. And after we were all made to wait around for a few minutes, in came Princess Kate and Prince William holding baby Prince George. They seemed very nice – George's mummy appeared to have a similar hair affliction to my mummy, i.e. too much of the stuff around the face that required almost constant flicking, and George's Daddy is going bald, but apart from that they were OK. But then I saw Prince George.

Now hang on a minute, I am all for meeting other

people in this big old world of ours, lord knows I have to do it enough of the time. And after meeting Adam I'd become rather converted to kids, as you may recall, and I think there may be a good deal to be said for having them around the place from time to time. But this was a different matter altogether – George appears to be another baby alright, but he's another baby who can do a lot more stuff than me. I mean, he can make sounds, he can crawl around the floor threatening the posh furniture, he can sit up – Sitting Up!! Who knew that was possible? Hmm, I'm not sure I like this at all.

Of course he also had on a personalised T-shirt, but his one said his actual name on it, not some bastardised shortening which his mum and dad were going to claim as his nickname. 'Oh yes, we call Eric just Ric for short sometimes,' I heard Dad weakly propose to obvious disbelief. 'Yes, and, well you know who uses capitals these days, ha ha!' he continued, while everyone wished he would stop.

And meanwhile, Prince George was getting all the attention, not me. No fair! He could do stuff, he could get around, he was entertaining. Now that I look at matters in the cold light of day I realise all I really do is lie around waving my arms and legs and occasionally demanding food with menaces. And when you think about it, that's not actually that diverting. Blimey, I'd better shape up and start doing some growing. I'll be needing more of the good stuff to do that. So, I made my feelings clear to Jeeves that it would be awfully decent of him if he could see his way clear to providing me with a bottle of m, and sensing my desire, he duly obliged.

I chugged it down while Mum and Dad and George's mum and dad got on with the tedious task of comparing what things their little one can and can't do, and what hilariously entertaining thing happened yesterday with a baby wipe. I had gulped down the whole lot, and while noticing that conversation had once more drifted towards the subject of Prince George and his subjects, and entirely away from the subject of me, I also noticed some rather peculiar gurglings going on in my stomach. What was happening I wasn't entirely sure, but pretty soon everyone found out.

To the cry of 'Oh, my good Lord, no!' from Dad, I delivered an enormous projectile vomit of over-hastily chugged smelly milk. It was spectacularly vile! And it went right over the posh furniture, right over the crest-emblazoned rug, almost over the precious boy Prince himself, and certainly right over Mum and Dad's pride. Totes hilaresballs!!! While the grown-ups screamed and apologised in turn, and while servants dashed in to attempt to limit the damage, and while Wills and Kate muttered excuses under their breath and whisked George, and indeed themselves, away from the scene of the crime, I lay back in Jeeves's arms with the self-satisfied expression of a baby who has seen a job well done.

We left shortly after. We were not invited back.

Put it this way, I don't think Mum and Dad will be repeating their mistake of forgetting that I'm the one to watch any time soon. Smiley face!

Meanwhile, a few days later I discovered that it was possible to sit up and not roll over backwards bashing my head on the shagpile, as I had previously been wont to do. Yup, sitting up is actually dead easy, just as soon as you have the age for it. Aha, you won't catch me being outsmarted by a royal baby and the entire adult population for long.

Plus, I think we can agree that I can projectile vomit better then all of 'em.

BRITAIN'S GOT TALENT
- IN AMERICA

I'm talking about myself, of course – quite the smartest baby, I think you'll agree. And it's not all about Jeeves in the background being the puppet master and pulling my strings with effortless superiority. No, I am fully in control of my destiny whatever Nanny Sharon might say about me 'getting a bit fractious towards the end of the day and needing to be put down for quiet time'. Good, so long as we've got that straight, as I said to Nanny Sharon. She replied, 'Time for your quiet time, Eric', which didn't really back up my point, but I maintain my baby independence nevertheless.

But I digress. What I'm actually referring to is that

shortly after the fracas of baby George and his mum and dad (whether because of it or not, I'm not entirely clear) Mum took me back to America – without Dad! Shock, horror! I thought he said he loved me so, so, so much that he never wanted to be without me, and I was the best thing that ever happened to him, and I meant more to him than life itself. OK, he never actually said the last bit, but he definitely said the first things, and yet there he was, deserting me! Letting me go to a strange country I've never been to before (well, OK, I was born there, but I mean apart from that…) with only my mum for company! And Jeeves. And Nanny Sharon. And Pecial Blankie. And a hundred-weight of toys and clothes. OK, it's not too bad, I suppose.

But I still wanted Daddy to know I'm cross. So I spent a whole twenty minutes giving him the silent treatment the moment I heard about the plan, but it didn't really have the desired effect. At the end of it Dad said, 'Oh, Eric Werick (God, I thought he'd given up on that), it is just incredible, spending time with you. And you are the most amazing baby I have ever met (I don't actually think he'd properly met any babies before me, but never mind), you are so

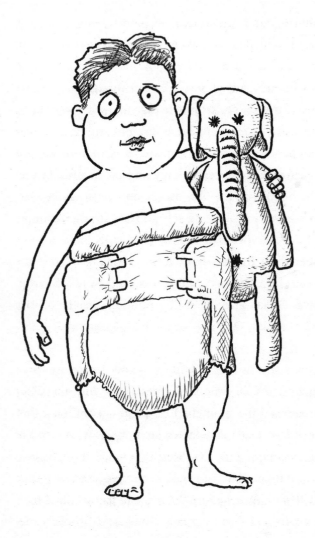

amazingly quiet. You're an inspiration.' Sometimes, I feel I'm really not getting my point across.

So, anyway, I had to go. We were going to stay in one of Mummy's houses in America with all of her assorted family again, and of course, as Daddy wasn't going to be there I would be able to see my brother again. Cool! Apparently some families live with each other all the time and the kids see each other every morning at breakfast and every night before they go to bed. I guess those must be the kinds of families where it doesn't happen that the mum and dad meet on the mum's husband's yacht, and when the mum's husband happens to be the dad's best friend, or rather Mum's ex-husband is Dad's ex-best friend.

Jeeves says that Tolstoy says something profound about families being happy or unhappy. I thought I might ask Dad about it one day, but Jeeves says there's no point because Dad wouldn't know who Tolstoy was if he bit him on the bum. I thought it was pretty unlikely that whoever Tolstoy was he would like to risk the wrath of my Dad when he had been bitten on the bum although that is something I would like to see, thinking about it. But anyway Nanny Sharon brought matters to a halt by interrupting Jeeves with the immortal words: 'Will you stop talking rubbish to Eric, Piers.' 'Never going to happen, Sharon,' said Jeeves, 'never going to happen.'

I don't want to talk about the journey to America, and Mummy obviously feels the same way because I heard her speaking to Daddy on the phone when we finally arrived at Mummy's house in Florida. 'Let us never talk of the flight to America with Eric that I had to cope with all on my own without you. I'll just leave you with this silence so you can imagine how horrendous it was.' But Daddy must have not heard the profound effect of the silence, mainly because there wasn't any as she immediately began telling him all about it. She made it sound like it was *my* fault – 'Eric cried for x many hours, Eric kept pooing uncontrollably, it was complete hell coping with a baby for hours on an intercontinental flight', etc., etc. I mean it hadn't been my idea to spend my life going backwards and forwards between England and America, had it? Isn't family life meant to revolve around the children, rather than around the Dad's obsession with showing off his teeth on television on a weekly basis? Nanny Sharon says it's like living with an addict – all the important and day-to-day decisions have to be about them – and I guess she should know.

But, I shouldn't complain, really. I mean, being in America did mean that I got to spend lots of time with Mummy. And it also meant there weren't so many cocktail parties every day, which was a bit of a bonus. But, get this – on only my second day of prime American relaxing with Mummy time, the nice routine of which I was getting rather fond (wake up, have milk, be entertained by my half-brother Adam, have Jeeves take me out for my daily post prandial, followed by more milk and then snuggle time with Mummy and bed. Sounds good, huh?) was rudely interrupted. By Dad, of course – who else?

First there were video calls with Dad. These involved Mum holding various electronic items in front of me while Dad waved and smiled at me in a kind of stop-motion animation sequence and I looked elsewhere entirely. But then we had an interruption of a grander kind.

It turns out that Dad is one of the judges of some TV show called *Britain's Got Talent* – who knew, right? And so we had to sit down as a family, with Jeeves and Nanny Sharon too, obviously, and watch the first episode of the new series. My favourite was the performing owl, but that is partly because Daddy named me after an owl, I think – the Eric Owl. But Daddy didn't like it. 'Sorry, it's over,' he said. A bit harsh, I thought. I also loved the Frenchman who played drums upside down in a giant wheel, but apparently no one else did. After that I fell asleep, so I'm not sure what else happened. I woke up to hear, 'It's four big fat yesses' and wondered why Daddy was saying that to me.

Only later did I discover the big swizz – not only was Daddy not talking to me, but that wasn't him talking at all right now – it was a recording, whatever that means, and Daddy recorded it before I was born. I must say I am almost entirely uninterested in things before I was born. In fact I'm not even sure they actually happened.

Hmph, it's a bit of a cheek, I think, that Dad should be back at home enjoying himself, showing off his new teeth and his old jeans while I'm out here with nothing exciting happening. Things had better change tomorrow, that's what I say.

SUPERSIZE ME

Wow, something seriously exciting happened today. I mean, wowballs! Harry Bighair and his friends came over to visit, but that's not what's exciting. What I'm talking about is the amazing new thing that Mummy gave me to play with today. It's, like, superfabmaniatastic! So, what happened was this.

I was having a nice little play with my toes – great things, toes, you can hold them, you can stick them in your mouth, they do everything! Anyway, there I was happily relaxing with just my thoughts for company (and my toes, obviously), when suddenly the grown-ups started acting all suspicious, furtively sneaking around me, muttering under their breath things like 'We don't want him to have a negative feeling

158

about it, we want it to be a positive experience' and other overblown Americanisms. What was going on? Then Mum advanced towards me, swooped down with a nervous air, and gingerly placed me in some kind of space-age plastic contraption with a cushion underneath me (looked like one of Dad's crochet numbers), and a cushion behind my head (definitely Dad's – it had 'Eric the Magnificent' embroidered on it) and said, 'OK, my sweety dumpling (groan), you have grown up soooo much, that now you are ready for…'

But I didn't let her finish the sentence. I could see there was something on offer on the table in front of me and it looked like my kind of thing. I picked it up and shoved it in my mouth just where my toes usually go, and – get this – it didn't just stay the same, like my toes do, and it didn't hurt my toes when I bit it, like with my toes. Instead it disintegrated; it rolled around inside my mouth, and then it disappeared. I'm not quite sure where it went after that but it seemed to reappear inside my tummy. I reached forward to grab another, missed, tried again, got it and repeat to fade. Eat, eat, eat, repeat. Eat, eat, eat, repeat. That's what I say. Yes, this was food!!! And damn nice it was too! 'Well, Eric seems to have got the hang of eating pretty quickly!' said Mum. 'The books say you should take it really gently and don't expect them to be ready for it, but I guess you're just a genius, my darlin' sweety pie!' Nanny Sharon muttered under her breath, 'These books don't know anything about what bringing up a baby is really like – the baby will let you know when they are ready, it's obvious. Been obvious for weeks that Eric was ready. I kept saying so, but did they listen, did they hell.'

But I was oblivious – grabbing rice crackers and stuffing them into my mouth was my sole concern. I have seen a lot of technological innovations made for someone of so few years (I don't have even one year under my belt yet, to be precise) but this food business – well, it beats them all!

I was still happily at it when Harry Bighair and his friends came round. Mum latched onto them and squealed, 'Look! Look! Eric is eating his first food!' Harry Bighair dutifully said, 'Wow', as is his wont, but I don't think his heart was really in it. I've noticed that people without children are a lot less interested in children than people with children.

People without children tend to see children as small poo generators, rather than as constantly evolving amazing miracles of nature. I think we're actually both – but I chose that moment to demonstrate to Harry Bighair only the first trait, leaving the second hidden, just for the moment. Yup, my first lunge at food suddenly had its inevitable effect and it was Harry Bighair's turn to squeal, 'Oh, Gosh Golly Goodness! Dear me, what is happening?'

Well, I should have thought that was pretty obvious, as it was happening all over Daddy's embroidered lace cushion, which incidentally I later discovered said on it 'Happiness is Homemade'. Hmm... Nanny Sharon swooped in. 'Too much, too fast,' she said. 'I said that from the start,' she added, even though she had said no such thing. Jeeves followed swiftly behind to attend to my behind, and Mum beheld the lace cushion, which now said 'Happiness is Splat'. Harry Bighair and all of his friends made their excuses – which went along these lines: 'We were only here to see Simon anyway, let us know when he's back in town, we don't really go in for scenes of domestic bliss and babies', which I felt was honest, and left.

I made a last desperate grab at some more of this food stuff, but it was never going to work. The grown-ups were too quick for me. They acted in a pincer movement, Nanny Sharon and Jeeves lifting me out of the chair to take me off to a secure environment, and Mummy removing the crackers from sight. No fair! Out of sight, out of mind, they say. You think? I think not. Until I find something else to distract me, it's food, food, food all the way. And I sure as hell was going to let these grown-ups know about it. With some morsels of crackers left in my mouth, I widened said opening and let out an unearthly howl of prehistoric magnitude, expressing the untold woe of baby deprived of thing baby wants. I was still going at it pretty strong when Jeeves found something to distract me. Probably it had only taken him about eight seconds, to be fair, but it felt like a lifetime of baby misery. I mean, wasn't it obvious that I wanted more food? Or was it obvious that I shouldn't be allowed to have any more food? Not to me it wasn't, actually. But to everyone else it was, and so the genius Jeeves found the one thing that could take my mind off it, the one thing that could genuinely distract me from my red mist of baby rage: he found a random plastic toy and put it in my hands. Clever stuff, this child-rearing lark.

Suffice it to say, the return journey to England was less traumatic for Mum – because whenever I started screaming blue murder she could shove some rice crackers in my hands or mouth to shut me up. But more traumatic for Jeeves, because he had to clear up the mess they made afterwards. Hey ho, it's swings and roundabouts, isn't it?

And so we returned to England, back to good old Blighty, where it rains, or the sun shines, and everyone constantly goes on about which it is doing, but it doesn't much matter to my Dad – you know he is going to take his top off pretty soon, whatever the weather.

PATCHING THINGS UP

Daddy's phone had been ringing out with its dulcet tones of 'So Macho' again and again today – i.e. another usual day in the Cowell household. Except that Daddy wasn't answering it. He was locked in his 'smoking' room with the strains of Mozart reverberating out, ignoring the phone ringing off the hook (not that phones have hooks any more, but you know what I mean), ignoring Ant and Dec's furious and piteous scrabblings at the door from the hallway, and also ignoring his only son's numerous waahing attempts to get his attention.

'There must be something pretty special going on in there,' Nanny Sharon said to me. Eventually he emerged, a self-satisfied grin on his face and a small quilt in his hands. 'Check this out, every-body,' he said, smiling broadly. And he proceeded to show us a patchwork quilt he had made, on which were spelt out the words 'Mozart Rules'. He then explained how every piece of patchwork was made with a different, meaningful piece of material – one was from my first babygro, two more were from tops that Ant and Dec had grown out of, another was from his own baby blanket, another was from his old school tie (on which he had embroidered the words, 'You don't think I'm so lazy or stupid now do you?'), and another was from one of Mum's favourite nighties. There then followed a short shouting session between Mum and Dad over his having cut up her favourite nightie behind her back and sewn it into a sodding quilt, and what kind of maniac does that? (The very nicest kind, I thought, but didn't say.) After this brief interlude, Dad turned to Nanny Sharon and Jeeves for their reaction. Or at least he would have done if they hadn't made themselves suddenly very scarce.

Then Dad announced that he would be away for a few days, at an annual convention of quilters near the pleasant market town of Bishop's Stortford. Mummy had a very clear reaction to this, and I can't say it was wholly positive. I think her words were something along the lines of 'You cannot be serious! You are going to leave me here with Eric screaming.' (I was not screaming, I would like to note – it was merely a low-level waah that I was producing. Although fair do's, I did have plans to work up to the full scream later, oh yes.) 'And with no one but your crazy showbiz friends for company (I thought this was very harsh on Jeeves, although pretty much fair enough on Nanny Sharon), while you go gallivanting off, fulfilling your insane sewing hobby! When will this obsession end? When will you see the light of reason? And above all, where's the money coming in? That's what I want to know!'

Dad replied to this request for information with a petulant outburst which ran roughly along the following lines: 'You don't realise what it's like for me! It's all Simon Cowell thinks this, Simon Cowell is going to be doing that... The paparazzi are always all over me for my slightest move! And it means that what I really want to do, what my passion is, my sewing, is something I have to do in secret. Only you guys know about it, and if word ever got out, I would be a national joke. This is the love that cannot speak its name. And the fact that I have to hide this love, that I must disguise who I really am, and instead be the public face of Mr Nasty is hard. *Really* hard!'

He continued: 'But when I am with the Patchwork Guild I can be myself. They are my true friends. They are the ones who have helped me through the hard times in my life. They are the ones who have nurtured my talent through the years, ever since I sent them my first rough needlework at the age of eight, it is they who have guided my course through life, and saved me from the abyss of depression countless times when I thought my sewing wasn't good enough. They are the ones who really, really know me. I am talking about Norah, about Enid, about William, and of course, Doreen. What I have with you and Eric, and Alesha and Cheryl and Ant and Dec is one side of me, a very important side of me, of course. I love you, darling, and want to spend the rest of my life with you but don't make me cut away the part of me that has always been there, that has steered my life and made me whole. Please, I beg you, don't make me abandon the Guild and my annual sanctuary at Bishop's Stortford! Don't make me give up my sewing!'

Well, I think it's fair to say that Mum was pretty much beaten down by this heartfelt plea. What could she do? She let him go. And she made Jeeves and Nanny Sharon sign some pretty aggressive Non-Disclosure Agreements.

So for the next few days the house was quiet. No Debussy, no Bartók, no Jancek, no Mozart, no 'So Macho' ringtones, and no thousands of people dropping in 'just to say hi'. Ant and Dec were pretty distraught and kept trying to sleep on Jeeves's head to make up for Dad's absence. Jeeves was not impressed by this behaviour, and encouraged them to make for Nanny Sharon's barnet instead, but she was having none of it. AntandDec themselves (whom I decided not to call Squiddly and Diddly any more because it was seriously confusing me) popped round once, and everyone made different excuses as to where Dad was. They obviously knew something was up, so Mum said

Dad was having an affair and that seemed to put them off the scent.

Just when I was beginning to give up hope of ever seeing Dad again, suddenly the house was lit up with the blinding flash of sunlight reflecting from his sunglasses and teeth – he was back! He seemed in a very good mood, and I was glad to see him, of course. I showed my pleasure by waving my arms and legs even more enthusiastically than usual, so much so in fact that Mum said, 'Look, Eric has learned how to wave hello!' I hadn't, but you have to let grown-ups have their little delusions, don't you?

I must say, however, that I did rather share Mum's feelings on the subject of Dad's sewing, and so I was rather appalled that he had abandoned us for the sake of some old biddies and their patchworks. But then Dad did something that made me entirely forgive him. To the cry of 'Look what I've brought for Eric!' he produced a pair of baby sunglasses, and my very own baby-sized car, saying 'Eric 1' on the number plate. Now that's what I'm talking about! Say what you like about trashy celebrity culture, but this is just downright cool.

Turns out he had bought Ant and Dec matching sunglasses, too – wow, we are going to look pretty mental going to the park together.

LOOKING PRETTY MENTAL GOING TO THE PARK TOGETHER

Yup, we sure did! Oh, my lord, we Cowells really know how to draw attention to ourselves!

So first there was the usual three-hour palaver of getting out of the house, the responsibility for which Daddy sloughed off onto Jeeves by slipping into his smoking room for a bit of quiet needlework while listening to Brahms and casually calling out to Jeeves, 'I'm awfully busy at the moment, call me when Eric and the dogs are all ready to go.' Mummy and Nanny Sharon were nowhere to be seen, having clearly decided they wanted nothing to do with this madness. So, after a cavalcade of chasing round for nappy supplies, putting all the matching clothes

172

and sunglasses onto me and Ant and Dec, and then chasing round clearing up after weeing dogs, not to mention weeing babies, Jeeves was finally ready to call Dad.

Dad emerged, carrying a very pretty little lace number upon which he was stitching many tiny-petalled flowers with a combination of feather and chain stitches, using thinned-out embroidery thread in contrasting shades of scarlet and eau de Nil. WAIT UP! What's happening here? I seem to be learning about sewing through osmosis! This is totes not the plan, bro! Major mental note to self: just because sewing is Dad's obsession it does not have to be mine, no way, no how! I averted my eyes and got back to the matter in hand, trying to leave the house, and fortunately Dad did the same. He bit the thread with his shiny teeth, created a tiny knot with his large hands, and carefully placed the lace contraption under a telephone handset unit, adjusting the two until the handset sat just perfectly upon the lace doily. After a last parting glance at his creation (good grief!), he finally got with the programme by putting on his sunglasses and announcing, 'OK, we're shipping out.'

I was sitting in my very own car, Eric 1, safely strapped in with the many adjustable straps, which it is every Jeeves's duty to know inside out. I was wearing my 'I'm Simon Cowell's top dog' tee, and I was wearing sunglasses too. Ant and Dec were also wearing their matching top-dog tees, and they were attempting, mostly unsuccessfully, to wear sunglasses too, but they weren't on leads. What was all that about? I have to be held in with safety straps aplenty but they get to roam free. Why so? And how was this car going to move anyway? I mean, there were pedals down there but there was no way I was going to try to push myself along with them even if I could reach them, which I'm not sure I could, if I really tried. OK, I'm sure I couldn't, even if I really tried.

Well, it turns out there are usually two ways that a car for a baby is made to move along the street by a parent with more money than sense: one is to push the car by means of a pushing stick, like the handles of a buggy. This method has the advantage that the parent is in control – often a good idea – and the car never goes too fast, or in the opposite direction to where the parent is trying to go. But it

174

has the disadvantage that the parent has to get stuck in with the pushing process, get their hands dirty if you will, not something my Dad is usually keen on. So, there is the other, more technological, solution. This is called Remote Control Baby and it really exists, I kid you not. In this method the 'responsible adult' carries a remote control unit and directs their son or daughter and heir's vehicle around London's pavements by just twiddling knobs and turning levers as if they were something you might buy at Hamleys. This has the advantage that the parent gets to play with a fun toy while pretending to bring up their child sensibly, but has the disadvantage that it is OBVIOUSLY MENTAL.

However, you may not know that there is a third way to propel your baby through the streets of the capital in their own Ericmobile. And it is this: after placing said baby in car and strapping in, you take a small dog and place it on one pedal, take a second small dog and – you get the idea. Yup, really. Did you really think that my Dad would be content with just pushing me along, or just remote controlling me down the street? Nope, doggy power, that's the way to go. And so, he spent a happy twenty minutes' walk saying, 'Come on, Squiddly, come on, Diddly!' and training small bundles of fur at my feet to press down on pedals alternately. It was very slow progress, but Ant and Dec seemed to quite enjoy it, and it certainly caused a major stir on Twitter, which made Dad happy.

Of course eventually Ant and Dec got tired and decided to wee all over the pedals instead, so Dad stuck them in my bonnet with their little snouts peeping out and tried remote controlling us the last 100 yards to the park. But after a near miss with a very surprised old lady he had to resort to the old stick-pushing method. This clearly got him down a bit, so he took his top off to cheer himself up. Finally, after what seemed like several hours later, we arrived at the park, which is a mere five-minute walk from our house. And what did we find there? Well, the paps, of course, goes without saying, but also all the lovely birdsong (largely drowned out by constant camera clicks) and... a novelty act that looked like it really was novel.

Just as we entered the park a lady came up to him and said, 'Hello, Simon, my dog can play the guitar, would you like to see?' Well, it turned out Dad really did want to see and he wanted me and Ant and Dec to see, too, so we all looked on in eager anticipation.

DOG VERSUS GUITAR

Quite a crowd started to gather to watch this spectacle, and everyone was thinking, Is this dog really going to play the guitar? I haven't seen Daddy get so excited since he heard the Matisse cut-out exhibition was coming to town. He quickly got on the phone and told a bunch of his friends and all of his twits about it. Soon the real AntandDec came by and ran around and squealed, 'What? What?' (they had one 'what' each, you see) Is the dog really going to play the guitar, like? No!' They also wore matching suits, I noticed. Perhaps they could swap with my Ant and Dec and push the pedals on my car on the way home?

Well, the lady began by whipping up the crowd

into almost a state of delirium by taking the time to take a small orange rucksack off the dog's back and remove from it a collection of various assorted pink lace items, which she proceeded to dress the dog up in. I wasn't sure exactly how this would generate the sense of enthusiasm in the crowd she was looking for, nor how it might help the dog to master the technical skills required to strum a guitar, but perhaps we would find out. AntandDec opined that the dog 'didn't look too impressed, like', but now that the dog was dressed up like another much bigger dog's dinner, lady and dog were both ready to go.

So, with everyone in a state of heightened anticipation, the lady sat down on a handy bench and started playing the guitar and singing. The dog did nothing. I mean, literally nothing! No, hang on, that's not right – the dog began walking away! AntandDec started laughing and so did the crowd but Daddy was getting visibly upset – he wanted to see a dog playing the guitar! 'She will, she will!' insisted the lady, who then called the dog back, and with her frilly pink hairbow flopping about on her head (dog, not lady), she came back and swiped at the strings with a paw. 'Is that it?!' asked Daddy collapsing into laughter, too. 'No, no,' said the lady, 'she can do much more than that!' and she grabbed the dog's paw and brushed it up and down over the strings. AntandDec resorted to extended scenes of guffawing, and Daddy joined in, but you could see he was hiding deeper emotions too: 'I genuinely thought the dog was going to play the guitar!' he said, rather piteously, 'I really, really did! I have to say, I'm really disappointed.'

Well, the dog was clearly not going to play the guitar, so we left the lady and dog to carry on with their lives of delusion and dog food, and Daddy took us away from the scene, after the inevitable several hundred photos taken of him with his top off, standing next to me in Eric 1 and our Ant and Dec squabbling in the bonnet. The real AntandDec mumbled, 'Well, if there are no guitar-playing dogs around here, we're off, like', and Daddy called Jeeves to come and bring us all home in the real car. I think Daddy was afraid that if he tried to extricate Ant and Dec from the bonnet of my car he would find they had hidden some treasure that he wanted Jeeves to deal with rather than himself.

And so we went home. But Daddy slipped away, leaving us in the car with Jeeves. I found out later when everyone thought I was asleep that he had gone into a music shop and bought two identical harmonicas and was trying to train Ant and Dec to succeed where the lady and her dog had failed. I'm really not sure that Britain has got that much talent…

But perhaps Austria has? I was about to find out, as the next night was a big party at our house to watch Eurovision. It had to be a secret party, though – organised by Jeeves with help from Ant and Dec (well, obviously they didn't help, just started weeing everywhere and saying, 'Alright, like') – and kept entirely secret from Daddy. It seems that Daddy doesn't like the Eurovision Song Contest. He says it's 'just appallingly trashy telly, where all the performers have about as much charisma as wax dummies, and as much Latin flair as polar bears, and the whole thing is just designed to appeal to the lowest common denominators in all of the countries of Europe and so-called Europe.'

'Jealous, moi?' I thought to myself, but said nothing. Mind you, that's partly because I still haven't learnt how to talk.

IT AIN'T OVER TILL THE BEARDED LADY SINGS

OMG Eurovision is great, isn't it? I mean, obviously it's totally ridiculous, but you've got to admit, whether or not you enter into the spirit of the thing, and I recommend not, it's dead funny. Thus it seems to me that the way it works is this. Every country to the west of China and to the east of America picks a song and a singer that is going to appeal to all the other countries. There is no point appealing to their own country because they can't vote. So, all the non-English-speaking countries sing in English (except for France, of course, who always insist on singing in French, because Marie Antoinette said 'Let them eat gateau' or something).

The song has to be new, but the singer can be old, like Bonnie Tyler. The performers must be aged at least sixteen, which is understandable, but don't have to be from the country they are representing, which is hilarious. This is why Canadian Céline Dion won for Switzerland. So, why can't my Dad persuade Justin Bieber to do the UK entry and then we can actually win for once, I want to know.

All the East European countries vote for each other, nobody votes for Russia because they invaded Ukraine, although what that has to do with the merits of singing twins with entwined ponytails, I don't know. At least one of the Scandie countries will perform a major heavy rock tune which is air-punchingly good and which no one will vote for. All the acts will spend thousands on setting off complicated sets of fireworks, which really have very little to do with singing.

One or two countries will submit ridiculous novelty acts; that honour this year went to France with a song that involved constant repetition of the word 'moustache' to supposed comic effect. People all round Europe will hold Eurovision parties, the aim of which is to laugh at the acts, and especially laugh at the people who report the votes from each country. It is true that sometimes these guys are the funniest part of the evening – how do you get to be one of those anyway, I want to know. Maybe Dad can fix me up doing that? I suppose it's not a very full-time job, though. All they're tasked with doing is saying hello and reading out three numbers, and yet somehow lots of them manage to spin this process out to several minutes. They also often dress up in the most extravagant outfits for those few seconds of dubious fame. Meanwhile, behind it all, is Graham Norton, doing jokes that are almost as funny as Uncle David's, while all evening long people say 'douze points' to each other in silly accents and fall about laughing.

Then what happens at the end is that the group who has had a number-one hit with the song right across Europe is the one that wins, and whatever the UK entry does, everyone spends the next several weeks bemoaning how hopeless it was and how everyone has got to pull themselves together and produce something better next year while secretly hoping we never win because it's too expensive to host the following year. Sounds great, doesn't it?

Well, I loved it, and so did Jeeves and Nanny Sharon. AntandDec came over, too, because this was the one television programme they don't present, and of course our Ant and Dec spent the entire evening gnawing on furniture and fetching people slippers they didn't want. But we had to keep it all a secret from Dad, and that was the tricky bit. Jeeves masterminded it – the word he put out was that Nanny Sharon's husband was holding an Alcoholics Anonymous meeting at our house at the time that just happened to coincide with Eurovision. So all my favourite people came to the door, most of them in clip-on beards, a genius idea that – it looked like they were in disguise (to keep the alcoholics bit anonymous from their significant others, the story went), but actually it was to get in the Eurovision spirit. Then Jeeves showed everyone into one of the 'meeting rooms', which of course also had a big telly, and Geneviève cooked up a storm with all varieties of party food, and sneaked in some alcohol for those who weren't fussed about being anonymous. David was there, and Cheryl, 'Why aye, man'ing' away for all she was worth, and Nanny Sharon had brought several of her (exceptionally loud) children. Even Granny England was there, but Daddy didn't suspect a thing. Her beard was particularly black and bushy and it fooled Dad straight off.

It was a really fun evening. The best bit was just when we thought we'd got away with the whole thing, and everyone had checked they had voted with their phones and were triumphantly singing 'Rise like a Phoenix', suddenly... in walked Dad. OMG. He was not happy. He let out a stream of invective, which I didn't think even Nanny Sharon was capable of. He talked about betrayal, about disloyalty on a massive scale. He asked if One Direction and JLS meant nothing to us. He told us that we had let him down, let the music industry down, and, like the inflatable boy found with a pin in the inflatable school, worst of all we had let ourselves down. When he spotted his mum in the corner – she had put her beard back on but it wasn't going to help her now – he said 'Et tu, Brute?' with horror in his voice. And then he saw me. I was waiting for 'Et also tu, Eric?' but instead he just turned away with an air of crushed solemnity, calling to Ant and Dec to come with him. We knew he planned to put them on his head and go to bed, hoping this would take his despair away (it's OK, it was the canine Ant and Dec, not the human ones).

Jeeves turned off the television. David made as if to remonstrate to Dad, but Nanny Sharon pulled him away, shouting, 'Leave it, Dave, he's not worth it!' Cheryl, AntandDec and Granny England sloped out and made their way home. Then Jeeves turned to me with a cheeky grin: 'Hey, we're in the doghouse now, my son, but it was worth it, Eric, wasn't it?' he said. It sure was.

THE PARTY'S OVER

I woke up today to find Dad sobbing uncontrollably. Had Ant and Dec weed on his head again as he slept, I wondered? But no, it was something more serious: he had been told that his hit musical, *I Can't Sing*, wasn't a hit any more and it was going to close. He had confided in me, and all the national newspapers, in case anyone had forgotten, that it had been like his second baby of the year – bit of a cheek that, but I'll let it pass. So, anyway, he was pretty upset. But being my Dad, he didn't stay that way for long. Oh no, he pulled himself together, got talking on the phone to everyone he had ever met, and came up with a plan. What better idea to cheer him up from the news of losing the show, 'his baby', than to celebrate his actual baby, i.e. me! Or rather, to celebrate him having had the brilliant idea of having me and being my father. 'I'm literally making this up as I go along!' he said – no kidding. Yup, there and then he planned a party for Father's Day to end all parties for Father's Day. I'm not sure other parties are held for Father's Day, so this could be a first.

He really went for it – suddenly the garden filled up with mini ride-on real steam trains running on real track, bumper cars with personalised number plates for all the celebrity kids who were going to show up, water fountains that spelt out the words 'Simon Cowell is Ace' when looked at from a helicopter, a helicopter, and a massive bouncy castle in the shape of Ant and Dec. I mean Squiddly and Diddly, of course – not the real Ant and Dec, that would be horrible. The garden is not actually that big, so it was a bit of a squeeze, I have to say.

Meanwhile, Geneviève got busy hiring an entire army of kitchen staff and they set to making father- and kid-themed canapés – yup, we're talking fish fingers dipped in Angel Delight, and chip pizza butties. Yes, I agree, they do sound horrible, but Dad likes them so he figures other people do too.

Drinks were relatively normal – Cristal champagne for the grown-ups, and Irn-Bru for the kids – getting back to his roots, said Dad. Getting everyone crazy high on sugar and alcohol, said Nanny Sharon, but no one listened.

Then the people started showing up, with bored-looking kids in tow. 'Why do we have to go to some party to meet kids who aren't my friends just because someone even more famous than you asked us?' you could sense all the kids had asked their dads after being squeezed into cars and driven for hours to our house. Well, they didn't stay bored-looking for long – as soon as they saw the garden their eyes popped out of their heads and straight away they got stuck in to the bumper cars, the bouncy castle and the water fountains. The helicopter was a bit of a mistake, I think – it couldn't actually take off without cutting off the heads of several party guests, which, while you might think this was a justifiable action, wasn't actually what my dad had in mind when he ordered it. Of course the kids would all be alright as their heads wouldn't reach the height of the blades, but even so. Meanwhile, the grown-ups hit the Cristal champagne pretty hard…

Things got pretty lively pretty fast. There were Jamie Oliver's children who, when they weren't complaining that they didn't like the fancy food and could they please just have a plain ham and cheese sandwich, were going pretty mental on the bumper cars. Then there were the Jolie-Pitt kids, who were having a high old time in and out of the water fountains, trying to make them spell out 'Simon Cowell is Poo', and drinking too much Irn-Bru because they have never been allowed sugar before. I liked David Beckham's children – one of them said he wanted to follow in his father's footsteps and grow up to be a professional beard wearer. Gordon Ramsay arrived with all of his many children, and he and Dad had a competition to see who could get their top off quicker – Dad won.

But if we thought the kids were wild, that was nothing compared to the adults; you wouldn't believe what they got up to. Trying to take the helicopter for a ride despite Jeeves's strict instructions for them not to, loading too much coal into the steam train to make it go faster and faster, shoving children out of the way to squeeze onto the bumper cars and then ramming them into each other at ever higher speeds.

They were drinking too much Cristal champagne, for sure. You'd think they'd never seen a Father's Day party before from the way they acted. Mummy and Nanny Sharon both started getting pretty het up and began saying things like, 'Simon, you've got to do something! This is getting out of control!' 'Relax,' said Dad, 'you worry too much. It will all work out fine, you'll see.'

But it didn't work out fine... Someone, Bruce Forsyth, I think it was, jumped too high on the bouncy castle and caused the bouncy castle ear of Ant, or possibly Dec, to get spiked on the electric fence Daddy had put up to stop 'foxes' (i.e. neighbours) getting in. Adele, trying to be helpful, ran over to check the wiring (one of her hobbies, apparently), but a bottle of Irn-Bru suddenly got sprayed all over the electrics and the whole things started issuing major quantities of black smoke. The steam train was just passing by with Gordon Ramsay riding it; he yelled out, 'Yee haa!' just at the moment when a piece of coal that had been piled up too high jumped free and landed on the bouncy castle, which then began to smoulder and burn. Luckily, Katie Holmes and Suri ran to the rescue and with Gwyneth Paltrow and Apple they began instructing kids to run into the water fountains in just the right order to make the fountains direct towards the fire and put it out. It did mean the fountains spelt out 'Simon Cowell is Nuts', but I guess it was worth it.

However, the fire being out was not the end of the matter because the water had not only put out the fire, but also disabled the electric fence. Fearing a cavalcade of foxes, and neighbours, Dad suddenly woke up to the danger and called out, 'Help! Help!' Bruce Willis appeared at his side and started talking about taking them out with his piece, and to calm him down Nanny Sharon poured a glass of water over his head. Aunty Amanda turned to Dad and said, 'Press the reset button, that should fix the fence! There, that gold button there!' And everybody took up the chant, 'Push the gold! Push the gold!' Dad got the message and pushed the gold button. But nothing happened! No one was through to the semi-finals of life, the electric fence was still broken, and Bruce Forsyth was still stuck on a deflating Ant or Dec and no one was doing a damn thing about it.

Of course, everyone needs a Jeeves. And luckily we have one. In he strolled, masterfully in control of the chaos of the situation. 'What have you got, Piers?' asked Dad, 'I don't believe even you can fix this crisis.'

But he could. Of course he could. It was so simple, it was genius: he simply put on the largest television in the house, the one that takes up most of a wall, and then called out, 'Do come inside, ladies and gentlemen, boys and girls. Come and see what's on the television.' He coaxed them all in, quiet as lambs. Gordon Ramsay, Romeo Beckham, Poppy Oliver, George Clooney, Dannii Minogue, Joe McElderry, Rosie McClelland, Adele, Bruce Willis, and all the others. In they all came and sat down. Jeeves changed the channel from the final of *Britain's Got Talent* and instead broadcasted the lovely calming effect of pontypines, pinkyponks and ninkynonks. Yes, it was the children's TV series *In the Night Garden*, and it calmed everyone down something lovely. Funny how it works on everyone, no matter what age.

Jeeves and Nanny Sharon quietly organised the delivery people to take away all the helicopters and bouncy castles, and Irn-Bru and Cristal, and rounded up the valets to bring the cars to the door to execute a speedy exit for all the A-listers, the B-listers, the children, the wannabes and the has-beens. And they all went home.

Just another normal day in the life of a Cowell baby, apparently. Good grief, is this what I'll constantly have to put up with? Is there any hope of salvation? Will my life always be trending on Twitter?

THE FUTURE'S SO BRIGHT, YOU GOTTA WEAR SHADES

After the debacle of the party Dad was very busy. I hardly saw him for days at a stretch. No one knew what he was doing. Jeeves and I spent happy days during which he tried to teach me the rules of chess, and Nanny Sharon came by and said what an idiot Jeeves was. Ah, good times, good times indeed.

Finally, after days and days of this Daddy appeared and gathered us all together, the whole family – Mummy, Jeeves, Nanny Sharon, Geneviève and other assorted members of the household staff. Daddy asked Mummy to dim the lights and he put on suitable music – Verdi, I think. And then to a fanfare – metaphorical this time, thank goodness –

he brought out what he called his 'masterpiece'. Jaws dropped, eyes widened, eyebrows were raised, and people were generally knocked down with a feather. It was my own Dad, in his usual long stitched-up jeans and nondescript T-shirt, and he was carrying something: something very heavy, and very white.

He held it out for us all to see and admire. It was a wedding dress. A beautifully stitched, embroidered and appliquéd stunning white wedding dress made from exquisite ivory antique satin, complete with taffeta underskirts and a silk train. Perfectly sculpted and intricately sewn, it would be any bride's pride and joy. Mummy murmured, 'Oh Simon!' and gasped in delight. Then Daddy burst the bubble: 'Oh no, it's not for you, love! It's been made to order. It's for a Thai bride.'

Horror struck Mummy's face. Nanny Sharon went a shade of white I didn't know she was capable of, and even Jeeves lost some of his composure and coughed under his breath and said, 'Gosh.' 'No, no!' said Daddy, 'I'm still not planning on marriage any time soon, you know. This is for the business, for my passion, for Eric's future.'

Mummy uttered several quite extraordinary expletives and asked Daddy what the hell he thought he was playing at. Daddy got pretty hot under the collar and finally shouted, 'Look, I'm thinking of you and Eric here, you know! Of our future! When the music and telly business goes tits up, like the show did, I'll still have the Thai bride business to keep you in sun-dried ciabatta and guacamole! What would you do without the *Britain's Got Talent* and *The X Factor* money? Hey, have you thought of that?'

'Well,' said Mummy, 'I would probably manage to get by on my massive divorce settlement and my previous career as a rich heiress.'

'Oh, yes,' said Dad, 'I hadn't thought of that.'

So Jeeves intervened. He subtly turned off the music and undimmed the lights. Then he put something calming on the television while Nanny Sharon fixed Mummy a stiff drink. The staff melted away, sensing their presence was no longer required. 'Shall I put the dress away now, Sir's Sir?' said Jeeves quietly.

'Yes, Piers, thank you. Please do that,' Dad replied, somewhat dejectedly. He looked hopefully for forgiveness in Mummy's eyes and, luckily, he found it. And then they both remembered me and picked me up and we all sat down on the sofa in the small sitting room with the small television, everyone on everyone's lap, and watched *Peppa Pig* and played at being a normal family. It was good. It was maybe even salvation. Perhaps there is a hope of normality for me? Maybe I can escape from the social Cowell prison I have been born into, and grow up with a normal family life?

Well, you can't blame a baby for hoping.

And so, dear reader, we leave them. Happy in their little big world of Jeeves and Nanny Sharon, AntandDec and furry Ant and Dec, 'So Macho' ringtones, paparazzi, million-dollar jeans and T-shirts, sunglasses and 'why aye, man'. For, yes, the time has come for me to put down my iPad, stop dictating to Siri and continue the process of extricating myself from the rat race. Join me in a year's time to follow my further adventures in *My Life in the Media Spotlight*, or, as I prefer to think of it, *Help! I'm a celebrity baby… Get me out of here!*

BB4N, Eric.

XOXOXOXO